Secrets from the Sixth Floor Window
J.F.K. Assassination book

by

Connie Kritzberg

An Original Publication of Under Cover Press

Copyright © by Connie Kritzberg

Cover Design by Tom Keith

Page Design by Karin Loudermilk

ISBN: 0-9639062-1-6

Under Cover Press publication: October, 1994

10 9 8 7 6 5 4 3 2 1

Printed by Gilliland Publishing, Inc. in USA

Secrets From the Sixth Floor Window is dedicated to Samuel F. Kritzberg, my husband, best friend, and editor who said at various times during the course of this writing:

"Slow down, you're writing too fast...
"That sounds good...
"Editing is a tough job...
"Is this book ever going to be finished?"

ACKNOWLEDGMENTS

This book could never have been written without the assistance and support of others. Some are named in the text. They are the reporters in Dallas, Texas on November 22, 1963. All shared in Dallas' grief, in their own fashion. They have as many varied ideas of why President John F. Kennedy was killed in the city that day as other Americans. I salute them, because when we talked or corresponded, they earnestly tried to recall the tragedy as accurately as they could.

They have one vast distinction from other Americans who recall where they were that day. *The reporters were there.*

Then there are individuals of Tulsa, Oklahoma to whom I am indebted. Especially to Tom Keith, a knowledgeable researcher and the designer of the cover of *Secrets in the Sixth Floor Window.* Tom listened carefully as I explained how I envisioned the cover, the metaphor behind the title, and managed through his own artistry to transfer the thought into a book cover. I am sure that Tom will soon be acclaimed in the book design field. Karin Loudermilk is the interior design artist of *Secrets*, who has an additional talent. Her knowledge of computers and software is extensive. In my mind, when a computer balks, she snaps her slender fingers and the reluctant machine realizes it has met its master. Kim Kidd is always a careful proof reader. Any defects in that area do not belong to her, but to the haste in which this book was written and produced.

Craig Roberts, author of *Kill Zone* and seven other books, is an established author, and has as full a schedule as anyone I have met. Nevertheless, he led me through the publishing process, saving me endless costly and unnecessary steps. He also referred me to the right printing company for me.

Then there is my husband, who suffered with me as I encountered many stumbling blocks. He empowered me with his intelligence; re-established my boundaries when they loosened. He was my mentor, my psychologist in residence, and did it without mentioning the lack of compliments and expressions of gratitude when they were long overdue.

I am also grateful to Ian Griggs, who in the course of this writing, became a friend who shared my feelings about the assassination and gave me information and courage through his personal example. He and his fellow members of Dallas '63, the British Forum for Views and Research into the Assassination of President John F. Kennedy, have shown that new facts can be found, that we must all share our findings if they are to be of value. We Americans know the concept, but do not always practice it. Ian and company are setting an example for the American group.

Lastly, I treasure those researchers who realize that they have something in common with people like me, who have not, and may never reach their station. We are instead students of the assassination. Students can be a pain with our many questions, but unless you teach us, progress will be even slower.

To all of us who keep alive the question of who killed President Kennedy, and why, I give my praise.

EXPLANATION

Secrets from the Sixth Floor Window is based on experiences of the author in Dallas, Texas, including November 22, 1963. It is a study of the sociological construction of Dallas, and includes an exploratory section of docufiction, the "what if?" of an investigation by reporters the month following the assassination of President John F. Kennedy.

Jim Featherston, far left, watches the passage of President John F. Kennedy and First Lady Jackie Kennedy moments before the President was assassinated in Dallas' Dealey Plaza. Featherston was a Dallas Times Herald reporter. --AP Worldwide Photos

Contents

PART I
CARNAGE IN DEALEY PLAZA

Assassinate me you may; intimidate me you will not.

John Philpot Curran
(1750-1817)
Irish Statesman

Introduction

In the 1960's, most large cities had two major sources of news–a morning and an evening newspaper. In Dallas, Texas, the pages of the *Dallas Morning News*, the morning paper, were read to learn what happened the afternoon and night before. Others chose to read the *Dallas Times Herald*, the evening newspaper. The Herald carried news from midnight until noon. Although they were distinguished by their publication time, both papers covered the latest version of major stories, whatever their time of origin. Each revised editions during publication hours to include the latest financial information, international news and fresh crime stories.

Few people, except those inside the newspaper business, read both papers. In Dallas, Texas, the *Dallas Morning News* was published on good grade newsprint, holding more photographs and hard news. The *Dallas Times Herald*, like most evening newspapers, was heavy with display advertising and carried more feature stories.

Dallas residents, if they read the News, thought the Herald was "flaming liberal". Those who preferred the Herald considered the News "reactionary and right wing".

Although both publishers owned television stations, dominance by on-scene television news had not yet arrived. Although jokes were made about newspapers being something "to wrap the garbage in", they were closely scrutinized. An article was called a story, and many stories were carefully snipped from the page and dated to prove a point.

It was a romantic era for reporters. Some held star status; in close competition with sports stars. In the movies we were played by Spencer Tracy or Frederick March. Press cards could get a reporter in, while the ordinary citizen waited in line. We were given free passes to Six Flags Over Texas, and most of us attended the gigantic barbecue sponsored annually by the Texas State Fair. Most reporters tried to be as Bohemian as possible, while doing their jobs competently. The "who", "what", "where" and "why" had better be the way it happened, or at least written approximating the editorial point of view of their employer. Reporters from both papers were fiercely competitive. Surely, some News reporters were friends with those from the Herald, and vice versa, but we were generally clannish and fraternized with others working for our own paper.

There was a difference in working hours. The News staff finished in the late evening, but our working day usually was over by 5 p.m. Such separation produced a sense of group uniqueness. Unless we were all covering an important event, our paths didn't often cross.

I was first an obituary writer, covering feature assignments after the "obits" had been written and gone to press. Six months' later, the position of Home Editor became available and I moved across the newsroom to the women's section. I stayed at the Herald until 1965, then moved on to a small town paper in Oklahoma. Subsequent jobs included government public relations, a stint as a Congressman's press secretary in Washington, D.C., and two years as Managing Editor of *The Corpsman*, the national Job Corps newspaper. In this checkered career, I have covered the reporters' beats (titles associated with the field of writing) of obits, police, courthouse, Home Editor, Managing Editor, and reporter/editor of a small town's special section in a larger daily.

I was emotionally and psychologically engaged with the assassination of President John F. Kennedy from the actual day when I returned to the "cityside" (the hard news side, as opposed to women's news) to serve as an extra rewrite person. In 1993, a Kennedy researcher and I wrote, copied and sold a booklet entitled "For the Defense". *Secrets from the Sixth Floor Window* is an extension of that booklet, but this book deals with the reporters' roles and other relevant subjects.

To prepare for the project, I received assistance from several members of the Herald crew and even a cameraman from the *Dallas Morning News*. I corresponded and spoke by telephone to Jim Featherston, former *Dallas Times Herald* courthouse reporter. Jim Featherston recently retired from the School of Journalism at Louisiana State University. As a respected professor, he was honored by several news articles on his retirement. A scholarship in his name was established by his former students. Jim, a talented writer and a man with a contagious sense of humor, made a direct contribution to this book.

The other direct contribution was in the form of an interview with Tom Alyea, a cameraman/reporter for WFAA television, owned by the *Dallas Morning News*. Tom Alyea is retired and lives in Tulsa. He has contributed his independent article to this book. He was the first newsman to reach the sixth floor of the Texas School Book Depository. He garnered "riches" from that experience. I wrote to former city editor Kenneth (Ken) Smart now Editor of the Weatherford, Texas *Democrat.* Ken Smart recently transferred there from New Mexico in preparation for retirement. He and his wife plan to live permanently in Texas where they have family in residence. He answered many questions for me, especially regarding the rearrangement of the editor's section on November 22, 1963 as a "Presidential desk". He also supplied information about the reporters' assignments that day.

Keith Shelton is a professor at North Texas State University at Denton, Texas, and a contributor to the *Denton Chronicle*, where he was editor for a number of years. He was of great assistance by supplying answers to perplexing questions.

In Part I of *Secrets from the Sixth Floor Window*, I will endeavor to take the reader inside the newsroom of the 1960's to see and hear what I and other newsmen did when the unthinkable happened......when the President of the United States was slaughtered on a Dallas street. To accomplish this assignment, I have searched my memory deeply for images and sounds, which I will try to report, along with facts supplied by the newsmen mentioned above. We do not all agree, which does not surprise me.

None of us have forgotten the romance of being a member of the press in the 1960's; we hope we are able to help others understand some of our feelings, and deep commitment to the responsibility of newspapers in that era.

To overcome a possible communication problem, I am including a brief glossary. Medicine has its language; law its "legalese", and we had our own jargon. The glossary is as brief as I can make it.

NEWSPEAK GLOSSARY

Advance   A story written before it occurs, in anticipation of the likelihood of occurrence.

Assignment   Stories you are to "cover" (meaning go to, and write).

Banner   A story or headline stretching all the way across the newspaper; a big deal. Sample Headline: WAREHOUSE INFERNO KILLS 4 FIRE FIGHTERS, INJURES 10.

Beat   The reporter's area of assignment–education, obituaries, courthouse, general assignments, police or other.

Byline   When the story was well enough written or important enough to be attributed to the reporter; or the paper preferred to shift the responsibility to the reporter rather than share it.

Cityside   The part of the newsroom occupied by newsmen; where hard news originated.

Copy paper   Sheets of drab colored, inexpensive paper, bought in large enough quantities that reporters could use all they wanted.

Cutline   Description beneath a photograph which explains the content.

Dateline   The city of origin of the story.

Deadline   When every article to appear in a particular edition had to be sent to the composing room. No exceptions allowed.

Feature Story A story written with a human interest slant.

Hard news   Any news not written as a feature story, or by women, entertainment writers, or sports reporters.

Lede   The first paragraph of a story–the attention getter.

Lead   As spelled in 1963.

Morgue   The "library" of the newspaper, where past stories about major events or persons were kept in manila envelopes or files for our use in writing an updated story.

Newsman   A male reporter.

News-hen   A derogatory description of a female reporter used by chauvinistic men of the era.

Series   A series of articles written about a particular topic; usually five, beginning on Sunday and ending on Thursday.

Sidebar   Something interesting that just doesn't fit in a large story. Written in brief, the sidebar is placed adjacent to the major article. Example: Fire Marshal Investigates Possible Arson in Fire. (See Banner)

Slug   The word a reporter used to describe his story, often followed by a slant mark and the reporter's last name. Slugs were typed on each page. Example: "MOORMAN/FEATHERSTON".

Stop the
Presses   Something seldom done unless it is evident that if the story or mistake stays as written, the paper will go out of business or suffer consequences which give the publisher ulcers. If the order is given, the editor or reporter next worries if he will have a job the next day, because a press roll and the role of pressmen were far more important than any lone reporter.

Story   A newspaper article of any type.

-30-   In the 1960's, the symbol for the end of the story.

One

Triple Underpass... Shooting....the President

With City Editor Ken Smart's first blurted words, our small world changed. Each of us who were there have our own memories and I earnestly wish I could describe my own reactions in an eloquent fashion. I have a memory of a dark hole. For a few seconds, my fingers felt paralyzed, and the horror of being unable to type jolted me back to reality. The day had started so differently, full of excitement and expectation.

I began the day writing "brides" (stories about the coming wedding of anyone who requested it), at my desk in the women's section. In the afternoon, I was to work for City Editor Smart on "cityside"; the section where all hard news originated. I believe I received the assignment as a rewrite man largely because I was one of the few women who had ever worked on cityside–thus being capable of "thinking like a newsman". I was delighted with the assignment, regardless of the reason.

Some of the higher level staff, including my boss, the Women's Editor, had plum assignments at the Trade Mart where they were to break bread with President Kennedy and hear him speak. They returned to the newsroom later, depressed and dejected, not having had the opportunity to play their assigned parts. And I know their grief was also showing.

I was excited but not the least apprehensive. Granted, the scenario was an editing challenge...one that made the *Dallas Morning News'* situation a stroll in the park. They had all afternoon to work before their first Presidential edition–we had a half hour. For the reporter or rewrite person, the assignment that day meant fast thinking and typing. Two editions had gone to press, and the deadline for the largest edition–the Home Edition–had been rolled back to 1 p.m. from its scheduled time of 12:30 p.m. Essentially we were to write and edit most of an entire news section in a half hour.

The newsroom could have been the setting for a factory. Windows were only on the south side. Desks were gray metal. Telephones were mounted on the sides of reporters' desks with headsets, so our fingers were free to type. There were no paintings on the wall; linoleum covered the floor. The large rectangular newsroom was divided by a wide corridor without walls leading straight from the "public" entrance. Outsiders reached the newsroom entrance by elevators from the first floor entrance to the *Dallas Times Herald* building. The newsroom corridor led to the enclosed Dallas office of the Associated Press. The opening to AP was large and teletypes had been frenetically clicking all day. We were all acutely aware that the President was coming.

Women, who covered such subjects as society, clubs, fashion and food, were segregated in their open section at the south end of the newsroom. Across an aisle was the small entertainment section, business and sports. Sports Editor Blackie Sherrod was darkly handsome, and a damn good writer as well. We accused the sports writers of getting unprecedented perks, from trips to expensive sports clothes.

Down that small aisle occasionally dashed Jack Ruby, headed for the entertainment writers. Not on November 22, but often enough that I recognized him, always dressed in a business suit and snappy fedora. Ken Smart said that Jack Ruby wanted the paper to cover a march of "his girls" on a downtown street. Their appearance was to be dedicated to some charity. The editor declined.

The cityside area, where all real news landed, was on the north side of the newsroom. There were rows of reporters' desks–one of which had been mine as "obit" reporter, the beginning job for many new reporters. At the northernmost end were the photo lab and elevators which took us in and out of the building.

Granted, the first floor lobby had been glamorized with marble floors, area rugs and plush sofas. But the only time I ever really looked at it was a day when all reporters in the women's section gathered for a group photograph. It wasn't real to the reporters; we entered and left by service elevators leading to the ground floor and an open parking lot north of the newspaper.

To me, and I am sure to others, the newsroom was more enticing than any paneled board room or the executive suites upstairs, directly over our heads. We were where it all happened. Everything a Dallasite would learn entered that room; and each of us, in some way, were privy to the first knowledge of news. And, after all, even now, news is what the average citizen awaits each day, whether delivered in person, by newspaper or television. In the 1960's, news originated in the very room we occupied each day. Photographs were sized by cardboard photo wheels, which converted their actual size into column widths, and a second point gave the depth in inches. Each reporter had a ruler with pica as well as inch measurements, called a "pica pole". Editors designed a page, which was supplied with space marked where advertisements would appear. Once spaces were marked for photographs and stories, it was called a "layout".

After we saw it, wrote it, edited it, the news stories were sent to the composing room where the words were set in the lead letters. Wooden frames held a page of type. One was assembled for every page which would appear in the newspaper, following the layout (design) drawn by editors. Editors went to the composing room to supervise the actual construction of the page. Lead letters made up the stories.

Editors badgered reporters for "shorts"–stories three or four inches in length–and ten inch stories. Such stories were in demand to "fill holes" when a page didn't come together just as the layout depicted. Unfortunately, those were the stories we disliked writing most. They were generally rewritten from press releases which arrived by mail. In order to preserve the originality of the newspaper, they were not published as received. At least not at *The Dallas Times Herald.*

On the lowest floor were the giant presses. They roared as they rolled. The smell of printers' ink filled the high ceilinged room like an aphrodisiac, binding reporters and pressmen together as a team. Each team member had a part in creating the news emanating from the press room. Reporters often made excuses to be there when the order to "start the presses" was given.

The presses were quiet when I finished my brief lunch and promptly reported to cityside. Ordinarily my day would be over by 4:30 p.m., but not that day. The assassination changed the order and sequence of writing, editing and press runs. A special "presidential desk" had been created by adding several extra tables with single drawers beneath the top. Abutting the editors' station was the "rim"–a horse shoe shaped wooden table where telephones with headsets were attached, creating a "slot". Since it was a large common desk used by several persons, typewriters and telephones denoted the space where a single rewrite man sat. Additional rewrite men and copy editors were assisting the city editor in preparation for the upcoming deadline.

Everything possible had been done in advance. Jim Lehrer, the Herald's federal reporter, had written a story about meticulous Secret Service protection. It had been typeset. Keith Shelton was at the Trade Mart with the choice assignment of covering the President's address in Dallas. His advance copy had been received, the story written and set in type. It, of course, would never be published. Reporters, including Jim Featherston, courthouse reporter, were at assigned places along the motorcade route. Bob Jackson, the Herald's star photographer, was in a convertible disadvantageously placed some seven cars behind the official cars. Tom Dillard, photo chief for the Morning News, sat in front of Jackson. To have a better view, Jackson sat atop the convertible's back seat. Unfortunately, they could see nothing of the Presidential limousine until it turned at an angle to the convertible.

Veteran police reporter George Carter was at the police station to call in if anything should happen.

I sat on the rim directly facing City Editor Smart. Ken, Tom LePere, assistant city editor, and others began the process of taking calls from reporters stationed along the motorcade route from Love Field as it wound through the inner city and into downtown. The calls were referred to us for transcribing as dictated by telephone. My first call came almost immediately after I was seated. Vivian Castleberry, Women's Editor and my supervisor, had an "advance" story (stories written in anticipation of an event which would occur). As she talked, I rolled the dun colored copy paper in the typewriter and began to type: "Dallas rolled out the red carpet today for President John F. Kennedy..." There was actually a red carpet leading to the podium in the Trade Mart.

The hot line buzzed and Ken picked up the receiver. He listened for scant seconds, then cast the telephone aside. I looked straight into his eyes as he stood. Ashen-faced, he said, "Triple underpass... shooting... the President."

Immediately, every photographer still at the paper ran for the elevators and disappeared. It seemed that all the phones started ringing. I remember a reporter in the photo lab sitting on the photo chief's stool, making notes in a small spiral notebook propped on his knee. Telephones rang where I never knew they existed–even in a restroom, it was said. Earlier, I had anticipated a challenging half hour, but it instantly became a journalistic nightmare. I resented the *Dallas Morning News*, which had hours to prepare its Presidential edition. What I didn't realize at the time was that some of our editions with the massive black headline, **PRESIDENT DEAD**, would be selling on the streets for $10 a copy.

Nothing existed, it seemed, outside the rectangular news section magnetized by the city desk. Other editors appeared from nowhere, and with the appearance of Felix McKnight, the desk assumed a protected status. McKnight, the Editor in Chief, seldom entered the newsroom. He had offices in the executive suite, and subordinate editors went to him. Now, McKnight took charge. We didn't approach the desk; they sent the copy boys to us.

I was moved to a desk among the rows and my spot on the rim assumed by someone else. No one asked questions, we just "responded". The telephone bells began to sound like one continuous ring. The first hour was spent coping the best we could. By 1:30, Ken Smart had closed the switchboard to outside calls except from reporters. I believed the outside doors were locked. I do know no outside publicists strolled in; no strangers approached the city desk. It was an hour more before a few reporters began coming back from their assignments.

Paper—sheets and scraps—was everywhere. Copy boys told us what to slug our stories. (See Newspeak Glossary.) We were told when to rip our paper out of the typewriter, often a paragraph at a time. Then the copy boy would scurry to the editor assembling the story. We could only hope we remembered where we had left off.

I literally did not have time to look up at anyone passing slower than at a run, until close to two o'clock. When the chance came, I asked a passing reporter, his head down, "Is he dead?" Whoever it was just nodded. I *knew*, but had not heard.

Two

Famous Polaroid

I had a need to get every word that we heard over the telephone... every tidbit of every "story". I felt a sense of desperation. If we did our part conscientiously, it might reduce, in some way, the sins of the killer or killers. Not that such a feeling had any basis in reality, but still...

An editor asked me to take a call from "Feather" (Jim Featherston, courthouse reporter). I willingly grabbed the headset. I thought,–*type fast*. There was relief that Feather sounded breathless and almost as stunned as I had been a few minutes earlier. He had good reason. He explained that he was out of breath after running through the motorcade to retrieve a sack containing a role of film tossed from a convertible by Bob Jackson. As quickly as he had the film in hand, he heard the shots. Seeing a man he knew, he asked "What happened?" He was told about the shots. The friend pointed out Mary Moorman and Jean Hill, noting that Moorman had a camera and had been taking photographs. Standing off the curb, in Houston Street, Jim had only to run a few yards to reach them.

When I asked Feather how far away he was from the scene, he half shouted: "I was right there". He calmed down and asked me to take the story and give him a chance to catch his breath. I heard sounds in the background, and although he hadn't said what they were, I knew that others were converging.

Feather told me if I would take the story, he would bring the Polaroid photograph in later. For all either of us knew, the photo taken just as the President was hit in the head by a bullet or bullets, was the only one in existence. And it did take its place in the history made that day.

I understood the way Jim must be feeling. He had to keep his witnesses from others in the news field. When you've got a "hot" story, you don't let anyone else get it. From my own experiences, I recall driving at an unsafe speed to the county courthouse in a small town. I was to interview the captives of a six-foot-six kidnapper, who had stolen an older couple's car and forced them to drive across several counties. The kidnapper-thief had been apprehended and held in the county jail. When I arrived, I ran into the sheriff's office only to find they had disappeared into the blue. It was only to be a feature story, as the wire service had supplied the news story. A sheriff's deputy told me that a radio station newsman had taken the family to an office for an interview. I ran–and I do mean ran–six blocks, flung open the office door and yelled at the startled newsman–"You're not on a deadline but I am. *You get them next.*" The couple sat with docility until I had my story. I then ran three more blocks to an office where I knew I could use a telephone, and called the paper to dictate a story. Damn it, they were *my* story.

I knew that even for Featherston, a seasoned and experienced newsman, it would take quick, hard work to keep other news people away from Moorman and Hill until I had their story. Suddenly, I began to feel the pressure of getting a story from two women in shock who would soon be besieged by other newsmen. But "Feather" won. I finished my interview of Hill and Moorman before they talked to television crews. My first thought as Feather called Moorman to the telephone was, "find out how many shots they heard". Still, I knew that I had to take the required first steps–find out their names, addresses, where they were standing and what they saw. To blurt out: "How many shots did you hear?" might cause one or both to hang up. And, it wasn't good reporting. Moorman had clearly been affected by the scene. She didn't speak until I asked where she lived. I found out that she was a school teacher and resided not far from me in central Dallas near Northwest Highway. Some small talk reassured her. She loosened up enough to readily say she heard four to six shots. She said her eye had been pressed against the viewfinder and she hardly knew what she had seen until the film emerged from the camera. Even then she realized she had not seen any blood. She remembered that she sank to the ground or perhaps was pulled down.

Since they were in the same room, I talked first to Moorman, then to Hill, back and forth. Moorman seemed to agree that people were running up the "hill". At least some were, she said. Now the spot is called the "grassy knoll". When I talked to Jean Hill, it became a different story. Shots were fired by officers toward possible suspects. She and other civilians ran up the hill to assist. Added to all this, there was a fluffy white dog on the seat between the President and the First Lady. Although I doubted the possibility that a dog was in the Presidential limousine, I wrote the story as given. The role of the reporter is to tell the story others tell him; not to create the event in his own mind.

Both Hill and Moorman agreed that they heard Jackie Kennedy scream: "Oh my God, they've shot Jack." I changed "Jack" to "him" out of respect for the Office of the President. For that I do not apologize, as every other reporter did something similar.

When I felt it was safe, I asked about the number of shots. Hill said she thought "four to six" and Moorman repeated the number.

My story read, in part:

"Both heard a sequence of shots, saw the President slump over toward his wife, heard the piercing scream of Mrs. Kennedy...

'I took the picture at the moment the shot rang out,' Moorman said. She continued, 'President Kennedy slumped over in the car and it shows Jackie leaning towards him... I heard Mrs. Kennedy say, 'My God, he's been shot.' I heard another shot or two ring out and I turned to my friend and we got on the ground."

Both women told me they believed they were directly in the path of bullets. The story[1] carried the headline written by a copy editor

Assassination
Candid Snapshot:
Picture of Death

Three

The Entrance Wound

The second story I wrote bothered me for a number of years and might have challenged my veracity, had anyone been concerned about what we reported that day. It certainly worried me.

At about 3:30 p.m. one of the editors asked if I wanted to "talk to the doctors". Truthfully, I did not. I was not a medical reporter and might have had a struggle with complicated terminology. I shouldn't have worried. It was the easiest statement that came to me that day. Doctors Malcolm Perry and Kemp Clark had taken part in resuscitation and medical treatment given the President. Although Malcolm Kidluff, Press Secretary to the President, had announced the President's death, Parkland Hospital officials could not be sure the local press had been present and, therefore, allowed the Herald and the News to interview Perry and Clark by telephone.

Both doctors seemed recovered from the stressful hours, and Perry made more statements than Clark, although the few questions I asked were answered without hesitation or qualification. The only speculative matter was the time of death and finally Dr. Clark said, "We put it at 1300". Later, I realized the importance of the Last Rites of the Catholic Church. The rites were administered, and death was placed after that moment.

If Perry and Clark's statement to me had been allowed to stand as given, and reported, the history of the assassination would have been quite different. They agreed no decision had been made whether there were one or two wounds. Next, Dr. Perry said that the neck wound below the "Adam's apple" (the largest cartilage in the larynx) was an

17

entrance wound. If it was an entrance wound, at least one shot would have come from in front of the President.

Because of the importance of that story, at least to me, I quote the story as published:[2]

To President
Neck Wounds
Bring Death

"Wounds in the lower front portion of the neck and the right rear side of the head ended the life of President John F. Kennedy, say doctors at Parkland Hospital.

Whether there were one or two wounds was not decided. The front neck hole was described as an entrance wound. The wound at the back of the head, while the principal one, was either an exit or tangential entrance wound. <u>A doctor admitted that it was possible there was only one wound.</u>

Dr. Kemp Clark, 38, chief of neurosurgery, and Dr. Malcolm Perry, 34, described the President's wounds. Dr. Clark, asked how long the President lived in the hospital, replied "I would guess 40 minutes but I was too busy to look at my watch."

Dr. Clark said the President's principal wound was on the right rear side of his head.

"As to the exact time of death we elected to make it - we pronounced it at 1300. I was busy with the head wound." Dr. Perry was busy with the wound in the President's neck. "It was a midline in the lower portion of his neck in front."

Asked if it was just below the Adam's apple, he said, "Yes. Below the Adam's apple."

"There were two wounds. Whether they were directly related I do not know. It was an entrance wound in the neck."

The doctors were asked whether one bullet could have made both wounds or whether there were two bullets.

Dr. Clark replied, "The head wound could have been either an exit or a tangential entrance wound."

The neurosurgeon described the back of the head wound as: "A large gaping wound with considerable loss of tissue." Dr. Perry added, "It is conceivable it was one wound, but there was no way for me to tell. It did however appear to be the entrance wound at the front of the throat."

"There was considerable bleeding. The services of the blood bank were sent for and obtained. Blood was used."

The last rites were performed in "Emergency Operating Room No. 1."

There were at least eight or 10 physicians in attendance at the time the President succumbed. Dr. Clark said there was no possibility of saving the President's life.

The press pool man said that when he saw Mrs. Kennedy she still had on her pink suit and that the hose of her left leg were saturated with blood. In the emergency room, Mrs. Kennedy, Vice President Johnson and Mrs. Johnson grasped hands in deep emotion."

The importance of the underlined sentence influenced this writer's view of the accuracy of assassination evidence, and made me a skeptic from the first day. Controversy over the entrance wound still exists.

Note that Dr. Perry said that he was "busy with the neck wound". When I asked directly whether one bullet could have made both wounds, Dr. Clark answered: "The head wound could have been either an exit or tangential entrance wound." Dr. Perry added: "It is conceivable it was one wound, but there was no way for me to tell. It did however appear to be the entrance wound at the front of the throat". The physicians told me there were "at least eight or 10 physicians in attendance at the time the President succumbed."

A few comments were added, but none as significant as these. Dr. Perry's statement, repeated on television, made a case for a conspiracy of more than one person, or a shooter to the front of the motorcade. That scenario was, of course, not allowed.

After writing the article with statements supplied by Drs. Perry and Clark, I went on to other tasks, such as talking to callers about canceled events, and scanning wire stories for references to local events. I heard scattered conversations—"They don't know where Johnson is..." "They caught the guy who did it..." "Everybody's over at the police station..."

There was a comic opera touch added by the story of a busload of bewildered Washington correspondents who unloaded at the Trade Mart. They knew that something untoward had happened, but not what. Herald gossip was that the Washington group ran around asking each other what had happened.

Clearly, news people were no better informed than the general public. They had segments of the assassination story; no news stories gave a complete and accurate account. Judge Sarah Hughes entered Air Force One undetected; LBJ even traveled to the jet in secrecy. In the first few hours there was fear that a coup might be underway. But even when newspaper people were confident that it was over, others were not so confident, as I would discover a few hours later.

I, like others, was so busy with messages and writing additions and updates to other stories that the editors correctly assumed we could not obtain evening food. An industrial sized cart arrived piled high with sandwiches and hot coffee. We ate between calls. When the tempo slowed somewhat, I was sent out to the streets to do a mood story on the city. We already had a list of canceled events and other "closings". Now I could do what I liked best, writing what I saw and felt.

Four

Dripping Red Letters

Copy boys regularly delivered new editions to the corners of our desks, the only spot where papers were not spread out. We checked one source against another as we wrote. There was no time to actually read the new editions. We only had time to glance at the folded top half of the front page and then return to the ringing telephones. I saw the large two line headline–"PRESIDENT DEAD, CONNALLY SHOT" with numbed emotion.

There was no way to know how many late editions were printed. Changes and pages were rebuilt constantly. Ordinarily, we filled out a photo request slip to obtain the services of a photographer. Instead a new photographer, one whose name I cannot remember, came to my desk. We went down the elevators, and walked eagerly into the darkness of Dallas.

We went through the lobbies of the grand hotels–the Baker and the Adolphus. We entered cafe after cafe, stopped pedestrians on the street, and talked to counter men. A cold wind whipped around my stockinged ankles, pages of newspapers flew into the air and landed on sidewalks and streets. Still fired by adrenalin, my energy did not match the mood of interviewees. Their mood was glum or despondent.

I was struck by the wail of sirens when there was so little traffic in downtown Dallas that night. Mirroring the wail of the sirens, Dallas cringed, and cried in shame.

The photographer and I walked until we had sampled downtown, then turned down Commerce Street toward the bars. Unlike today, we had no fear of the seedier section, and unabashedly gawked at the posters advertising the girlie shows. Several of the clubs were open. We stopped in front of a dark, drab club, its lights out, and stared at the poster board taped to the window. In large red poster paint were the letters "C-L-O-S-E-D". The poster paint was still fresh. Apparently the sign had been taped to the door before it dried. The red letters dripped, another reflection of what had taken place on Elm Street in Dealey Plaza.

The feeling was unforgettable. I remember it as yesterday. I honestly cannot describe it more adequately than what I wrote less than an hour later. I acknowledge that the style is embellished with adjectives, unlike today's straight forward news. We still enjoyed words, similar to sampling the newest blend offered in today's coffee houses, smelling it, sipping it and rolling it around our tongues to reach each taste bud.

My story, not bylined, as few were that day, was written and printed as follows:[3]

City in Shock
Friday Night,
No Stars Shone

"There was no rain or stars in Dallas Friday night. Neither were there stars...inexplicably there were occasional streaks of lightning.

The wind was merciless...

It blew tattered newspapers, wadded up scraps of paper and some coin dots of confetti in a whirlpool motion across the nearly deserted intersections.

It was cold. But was the November night cold enough to cause pedestrians to hunch their shoulders and stand over the gratings in the sidewalk to feel the updraft of warm air?

ALMOST WITHOUT exception, the few who walked the streets of downtown Dallas carried a newspaper under their arms. They walked slowly, the movement of their bodies showing emotion when their faces did not.

Clothed in a neat business suit, a man turned to his companion and said, 'You are now standing within six blocks of history.'

More sirens than usual broke the silence. Most of the other noises were made by newspaper vendors shouting, 'President assassinated'.

BUSINESS IN THE restaurants was poor. And it started early in the day.

'My boss called me down early. He went home,' said a man behind the cash register at a Main Street restaurant. 'He said they were ordering food and then wouldn't eat it.'

'Now,' he added, 'they just aren't coming in.'

'They are scared.' said a cafe owner of his few customers. The patrons regarded each other silently, looking up quickly each time the door opened. 'And I'm scared too,' he added.

LIQUOR STORES weren't getting much business in the downtown area. 'Everybody who comes in is so sad, and all they talk is this terrible thing.' commented a counter man.

Private apartment clubs were closed for the most part, with many of the downtown bars closed or preparing to close by 8 p.m. There was no entertainment in Dallas hotels. Most patrons stared silently at overhead television sets.

Walking up to the burlesque house where she was employed as a waitress, a girl in white slacks looked at the red lettered sign, saying, 'Closed' with astonishment.

'I didn't think he would close for anything,' she said, then turned away.

It is possible to stun a city.''

The photographer caught a photograph of one man, his big hand gripping a Herald paper. Parts of the headline, "President Dead" were visible. A photographic cliché perhaps, but that is the way it was.

Not caring where we were, or realizing that we stood in front of Jack Ruby's Carousel Club, the photographer finished his work. I talked to the girl in white as he photographed the poster. We returned to the paper where I wrote my story and afterward, was told I could leave. Other editors and a few reporters were still at work.

Five

And on Sunday

Close to 9:30 p.m., I returned to my home, where my mother was watching my children, who were already in bed for the night. After she left, I eagerly opened the only edition I brought home. I had my first chance to read the Herald. First, I skimmed the running story written by McKnight and next did what every reporter does–looked for the stories I had written.

I read the Moorman and Hill story, worried about the "fluffy dog" insert, then turned to my story with Doctors Perry and Clark. With a fearful start, I saw the sentence, not written by me, inserted in the third paragraph. It jumped out at me: "A doctor admitted that it was possible there was only one wound."

Had I made some error in such a critical story? Had it been crudely corrected by any of the editors I knew? If so, why was the remainder of the story just as I had written it? Also, responsible journalists always attribute remarks to sources, which I had done. The sentence completely lacked attribution. Knowing how it felt to have my "heart in my mouth" or throat at least, I jumped up and phoned the city desk, still set up and working. While I am not sure today who I talked to, it was an editor I knew. I asked where the sentence had come from. He was matter-of-fact. "The FBI", he said.

I can say with conviction that we did not joke and play around with our stories. If a reporter made an error, he or she heard about it. If an editor made a change in your story, he told us why. That is the way it was at the *Dallas Times Herald* in 1963. Another fact caused me not to doubt the answer to my question. The addition simply was not a sentence a reporter would write. What physician? Just someone wandering by? And was the FBI at the newspaper so soon? Someone said they were at other media points, searching for film or photos of Oswald which might have been saved. That made some sense. Eventually I went to bed, but slept little that night.

The children and I went to church school Sunday and then home. Like most children who had been cooped up in a church where they had to be "good", they were hungry, and making life unbearable until I pulled the Sunday pot roast out of the oven. I missed the newscast that mesmerized millions, but quickly saw a replay. I heard the words that held all America spellbound – "He's shot. Oswald's been shot." Like most Americans, I watched trapped in time. Oswald, dressed in a dark sweater was led from the jail door. Then the camera angle changed. The view I saw that day was not the newsreel commonly shown today–a view from the front of the line. It was a newsreel from Dallas, perhaps KRLD, which I commonly watched, and it was played and replayed. Where it originated is speculation. It is not speculation to say that I saw Oswald's face from the crowd side. I have seen the view only once in recent years, and the newsreel was so grainy that I would not expect others to notice what I had in 1963. I watched as Oswald shot a single glance of recognition at Jack Ruby just for an instant, almost smiled, then faced forward again just as Ruby lunged forward and fired his revolver.

Thayer Waldo wrote in his newspaper, the *Fort Worth Star Telegram* that an ABC cameraman pushed a microphone in Oswald's face and asked, "Do you have anything to say?" Oswald's eyes turned toward the microphone and Ruby lunged toward him.

I do not believe that is what I saw. I believe I saw recognition. It remains a still photograph in my mind because it was so damned important. If I am correct, Lee Oswald knew the man who shot him and for that instant, showed no fear of him. I realize there is a question whether the FBI was at the Herald Friday, although an editor told me so. But I know they certainly were at the Herald Sunday. The desk called me at home before 1:30 p.m. When the telephone rang that Sunday, I knew who would be calling. "Connie, do you remember where you were last night?" an editor asked. Were we at Jack Ruby's club? The FBI wanted to know. This time the editor's hasty demand left no doubt about the fed's impatient presence. I said that I thought so, but wasn't sure. I admitted I hadn't noted the street address and suggested they ask the photographer. The conversation was quickly over. I heard no more, principally because the photographer gave the wrong address and the focus left us.

Full of a reporter's curiosity, I left the dishes and, with the children piled in the car, headed downtown. I parked for a few minutes under the Carousel sign, recognizing it from the night before. It was coincidence...just a fluke...but why had the path of a meandering newshound led directly to the door of the man who would forever cast shadows over the case of the assassination of President Kennedy?

I thought about the look on Oswald's face. In those moments I surmised that Jack Ruby was the man Oswald had expected to rescue him.

I probably parked before the club no more than two or three minutes because that is about as long as three young children could bear unoccupied time. It was long enough for a belief to solidify. Then as now I believed that Oswald and Ruby were connected in some way; that Oswald's glance was plain and inescapable. Also clear to me was that Oswald did not believe this trusted acquaintance would turn on him. Otherwise, he would surely have flinched or otherwise attempted to withdraw. Instead he took one more half step toward death. That stroke of fate or simply circumstance would not leave my mind. Why was my story changed? Why was Oswald left open to an assassin, as surely as if the handcuffs had been removed and in a whisper, he had been told to run. Like in the movies. But most movies make the scenes seem more believable.

The internal questioning persisted. What motivated Jack Ruby? Insanity? His persistent quest for attention? A hidden reason? Then, still an innocent, I started the motor and partially lulled my sense of frustration with the thought that the next step would be one or more investigations which would reveal the "facts". Of course it would be revealed how the police knew exactly who they wanted so quickly. The police would know why Oswald was so close to Ruby's apartment when he encountered Officer J. D. Tippit. They would prove that Oswald killed Tippit. How could Oswald have stood on the sixth floor in the book building totally undiscovered for twenty minutes or more and calmly take the most difficult shots to score three times. Or was it only once?

How was Connally hit by the same bullet...there must have been more. All would surely be explained. My impatience would be rewarded. The questioning, shared by many others, still persists.

Six

Direct Contributions

Through my contacts with other newsmen, I persuaded two to give direct contributions to Secrets from the Sixth Floor Window. I value them, both for what they contribute to researchers and future writers, as well as for offering differing points of view. Coincidentally, all our conclusions are different. Put together, we can study them for any commonality, and there is some. Also, they emphasize the chaotic conditions under which we worked and the "brick walls" we met in trying to relay news to the public.

A cover-up is acknowledged by almost all readers. However, there were actually many elements of cover-up, from bosses who squelched news stories, to deliberate distortions. I have described what I experienced. Here now are the experiences of two very different newsmen, both professional and dedicated.

I Was There...
By Jim Featherston

I then occasionally felt like Joe Btfsplk, the cartoon character who walked around with a cloud over his head. A number of times during my career, which spanned nearly 20 years, I found myself on the scene of a disaster or tragedy.

At the time, I was one of two reporters covering the Dallas County Courthouse for the *Dallas Times Herald*. I had been working on newspapers for 12 years and the Times Herald was my fourth one. I had covered a number of big stories, including a tornado in Vicksburg, Miss., the Emmett Till trial in the Mississippi Delta and the Little Rock school integration crisis. I had also survived World War II. I was 40 years old and a bit jaded.

At any rate, I wasn't too excited about the Kennedy visit. I had met Kennedy several years earlier in Jackson, Miss., when he was a Massachusetts senator. I figured the presidential visit to Dallas would be largely without surprises - that he would appear as planned in a motorcade in downtown Dallas, would make his speech at the Trade Mart and then fly off to the LBJ Ranch near Austin on schedule.

Besides, my part in covering the presidential visit was to be minor. I was to station myself at the corner of Main and Houston, which was outside the courthouse and near the end of the downtown motorcade route, catch a roll of film thrown to me by Times Herald photographer Bob Jackson and also call in to the Times Herald rewrite desk information about crowd reaction. No big deal, I thought.

At this time, another Times Herald reporter, Jerry Richmond, and I worked out of the courthouse pressroom along with two other newspaper reporters and five television newsmen from two Fort Worth-based stations. The pressroom was straight out of Ben Hect's and Charles MacArthur's "Front Page," with pinups on the walls and empty beer and booze bottles littering the tables - along with old newspapers, overfilled ashtrays, ancient typewriters and odds and ends of camera equipment. The atmosphere was downright unhealthy, although to us it had a certain charm.

Jerry and I would always come in about 7 a.m. and would be the first to arrive in the pressroom. On this day, I had been in the pressroom only a few minutes when Jerry walked in muttering angrily about those "jerks" who had anonymously distributed anti-Kennedy handbills in downtown Dallas. Jerry had one of them in his hand. It was captioned "Wanted for Treason" and had two "mug shots" of Kennedy, one in profile and the other full face, just as if it were a police poster.

Jerry grumbled even more when a few minutes later he discovered that our competitor, the Dallas Morning News, was running a full-page anti-Kennedy advertisement. This ad, bordered in black like a death notice, was submitted by a self-styled right-wing "American Fact-Finding Committee" and was sarcastically headlined "Welcome Mr. Kennedy to Dallas." It accused the president of selling food to communist soldiers who were killing Americans in Vietnam. It also blamed him for the imprisonment, starvation and persecution of "thousands of Cubans" and strongly hinted that Kennedy had reached a secret agreement with the U. S. Communist Party.

Neither Jerry nor I thought the handbill and ad accurately reflected the mood of Dallas but instead were views of the same extremists who had struck U. N. Ambassador Adlai Stevenson with a placard and spat upon him when he had visited the city a few weeks earlier. Dallas was a big, rich, conservative city and many felt Kennedy was far too liberal, but we felt the city was too sophisticated to dishonor the president of the United States.

Later in the morning, Jerry and I, along with a television reporter, Jack Renfro, sneaked down the street for a beer. It was, after all, a festive occasion - at least, that was our excuse for drinking before noon but, to be truthful, we used anything for an excuse back in those days. At any rate, we talked about the presidential visit and agreed unanimously that nothing really bad would happen. Maybe a few anti-Kennedy signs or perhaps a few boos, but nothing more than that, we agreed.

Along about 11 a.m., as I recall, Jack headed for Love Field where the Kennedys would be enthusiastically welcomed after their short hop from Fort Worth. Jerry then left for the Trade Mart where he was to be one of the back-up reporters for the Times Herald. I went back to the courthouse and checked out the district attorney's offices on the top floor. While there, I talked to one of my favorite people, A. D. "Jim" Bowie, one of District Attorney Henry Wade's top assistants. Jim also thought "nothing really bad" would happen during the Kennedy visit. Within a few months, Jim would help prosecute Jack Ruby for killing Lee Harvey Oswald. Jim Bowie later would be appointed and then elected a district judge. But before the decade was done he would die of cancer at an early age.

Shortly after noon, I went outside and took my place near the corner of Main and Houston to await the motorcade and Bob Jackson. The motorcade was to turn right from Main onto Houston, travel a short block to Elm and zig-zag left diagonally toward the Triple Underpass. The crowd had thinned out considerably in the Main and Houston vicinity, and many of the spectators were people who worked at or had business at the courthouse. I was wearing a press card, which was issued by the police, on the lapel of my coat, and because of this a patrolman permitted me to step off the curb to await the motorcade. I noticed that the skies had cleared after an overnight rain and a heavy overcast morning. It was a beautiful day, and obviously no rain would fall on this parade. It was windy, however.

There was excitement in the air as the motorcade approached, and I found myself getting caught up in it despite myself. When the presidential car passed, I found myself rubber-necking furiously toward Jackie Kennedy just like everyone else. I had to restrain myself from shrieking "Hey, Jackieeee!" like so many others had done along the motorcade route. I barely noticed President Kennedy or Texas Gov. and Mrs. John Connally.

Bob Jackson was in a photographers' car, which was seventh in the procession. As the photographers' car drew abreast of me, Bob threw the film at me. It was in a little paper sack, however, and a gust of wind caught it and blew it toward the other side of the street.

I ran through the motorcade to retrieve the film and then heard the shots. I really didn't recognize the shots as gunfire - I thought what I heard might be fireworks. However, I quickly realized something catastrophic had happened from the reaction of the crowd. One woman was hysterical.

I spotted a young lawyer named Frank Wright. "What happened?" I shouted. "I don't know, but a woman down there has taken a picture of whatever happened." Wright said, pointing toward nearby Dealey Plaza.

I ran to Dealey Plaza, a few yards away, and this is where I first learned the president had been shot. I found two young women, Mary Moorman and Jean Lollis Hill, near the curb on Dealey Plaza. Both had been within a few feet of the spot where Kennedy was shot, and Mary Moorman had taken a Polaroid picture of Jackie Kennedy cradling the president's head in her arms. It was a poorly focused and snowy picture, but, as far as I knew then, it was the only such picture in existence. I wanted the picture and I also wanted the two women's eyewitness accounts of the shooting.

I told Mrs. Moorman I wanted the picture for the Times Herald and she agreed. I then told both of them I would like for them to come with me to the courthouse pressroom so I could get their stories and both agreed. When we got there, no one was in the pressroom except a free lance cameraman doing some work for NBC. "What's up?" he said. "The president has been shot," I replied. He laughed, thinking I was kidding. But when I got on the phone and he realized I was serious, he ran from the room. The next time I saw him several days later, he was still running.

I called the city desk and told Tom LePere, an assistant city editor, that the president had been shot. "Really? Let me switch you to rewrite," LePere said, unruffled as if it were a routine story. I briefly told the rewrite man what had happened and then put Mary Moorman and Jean Lollis Hill on the phone so they could tell what they had seen in their own words. Mrs. Moorman, in effect, said she was so busy taking the picture that she really didn't see anything. Mrs. Hill, however, gave a graphic account of seeing Kennedy shot a few feet in front of her eyes.

Before long, the pressroom became filled with other newsmen. Mrs. Hill told her story over and over again for television and radio. Each time, she would embellish it a bit until her version began to sound like Dodge City at high noon. She told of a man running up toward the now-famed grassy knoll pursued by other men she believed to be policemen. In the meantime, I had talked to other witnesses and at one point I told Mrs. Hill she shouldn't be saying some of the things she was telling television and radio reporters. I was merely trying to save her later embarrassment but she apparently attached intrigue to my warning.

As the afternoon wore on, a deputy sheriff found out that I had two eyewitnesses in the pressroom, and he told me to ask them not to leave the courthouse until they could be questioned by law enforcement people. I relayed the information to Mrs. Moorman and Mrs. Hill.

All this time, I was wearing a lapel card identifying myself as a member of the press. It was also evident we were in a pressroom and the room was so designated by a sign on the door.

I am mentioning all this because a few months later Mrs. Hill told the Warren Commission bad things about me. She told the commission that I had grabbed Mrs. Moorman and her camera down on Dealey Plaza and that I wouldn't let her go even though she was crying. She added that I "stole" the picture from Mrs. Moorman. Mrs. Hill then said I had forced them to come with me to a strange room and then wouldn't let them leave. She also said I had told her what she could and couldn't say. Her testimony defaming me is all in Vol. VI of the Hearings Before the President's Commission on the Assassination of President Kennedy the Warren Report.

Why Mrs. Hill said all this has never been clear to me - I later theorized she got swept up in the excitement of having the cameras and lights on her and microphones shoved into her face. She was suffering from a sort of star-is-born syndrome, I later figured.

It was a wild and crazy afternoon. While we were in the pressroom, Lee Harvey Oswald, the accused assassin, had left the Texas School Book Depository where he worked as a stock clerk. He had aroused suspicion when he did not return to work after the assassination, and an improvised sniper's nest had been found on the sixth floor of the building. Oswald had first gotten on and off a bus before taking a cab to his rooming house in Oak Cliff, a section of Dallas west of the Trinity River.

Oswald's description had been broadcast to cruising police cars, and he was stopped by Officer J. D. Tippit while walking about a mile from his rooming house. When Tippit stepped out of his patrol car, Oswald killed him with four revolver shots and was later identified as Tippit's killer by eyewitnesses. Oswald ran into the

Texas Theatre about eight blocks from where he killed Tippit. He was spotted by a shoe store manager and police were alerted. The theatre lights were turned on, and police arrested Oswald after a scuffle during which he tried to shoot another policeman. "Well, it's over now!" Oswald shouted, then added: "I protest this police brutality."

Meanwhile, President Kennedy had been pronounced dead at Parkland Hospital about 1 p.m. About three hours later, Lyndon B. Johnson was sworn in as the 36th president of the United States by Federal Judge Sarah Hughes aboard Air Force One at Love Field.

That night I went to the Dallas police station where Oswald occasionally was hustled through the halls between interrogations. The hallways were crowded with dozens of reporters and cameramen who jockeyed for position each time Oswald appeared. The atmosphere was sometimes chaotic. As I recall, Jim Lehrer (now part of the MacNeil-Lehrer team on public television) and Warren Bosworth were covering this scene for the Times Herald and I left because there was nothing for me to do.

I ended up my long workday about midnight back at the courthouse pressroom sharing a bottle of booze with Jim Koethe, a friend and fellow Times Herald reporter. Jim filled me in with information I didn't know about Oswald. I also remember his telling me about the many coincidences of the Kennedy and Lincoln assassinations - that both men had vice presidents named Johnson and that Lincoln had a secretary named Kennedy and Kennedy had a secretary named Lincoln and so on.

Jim Koethe himself would die a violent death within a few months. He was found murdered in his apartment, and police theorized he was the victim of strangulation or a karate chop. The case was never really solved, and his death has been linked with a conspiracy theory that contends an inordinate number of persons (more than 30) with direct or indirect connections with the Kennedy assassination died violent or unexpected deaths. The taxi driver, for instance, who drove Oswald to Oak Cliff was killed in a car accident, and one of Jack Ruby's nightclub strippers was murdered.

The next day was a Saturday and many people appeared at Dealey Plaza near the assassination site. Some were mere curiosity seekers, but many were genuinely grieved. Some brought flowers, which they left on Dealey Plaza in tribute to the slain president. I spent the entire day at the courthouse and around Dealey Plaza.

I interviewed Henry Wade, another of my favorite people who is still district attorney in Dallas. He said that oddly enough there was then no federal law against killing a president and that Oswald was to be tried in state district court in Dallas unless there was a change of venue to another Texas city. He also indicated that Jackie Kennedy and Lyndon Johnson, among others, probably would have to return to Dallas to testify at the trial. This, of course, all became academic when Oswald was killed by Jack Ruby. And now, of course, there is a federal law against killing a president.

Robert Oswald, Lee Harvey's brother, came by the district attorney's office at Henry's request, and I tried to interview him. The brother, who seemed like a nice guy, was a junior executive for Acme Brick Co. in nearby Denton and really had not been around Lee Harvey much in recent years. He pleasantly but no less firmly refused to answer any of my questions. Robert Oswald, by the way, wisely kept this mouth shut for a number of years. He finally agreed to an interview with old Look magazine.

As the day wore on, a crowd began to collect behind the courthouse on the Dealey Plaza side of Houston Street. The rear entrance to the county jail was across the street, and many were expecting Oswald to be transferred from the city jail that day. Undoubtedly, they were there in hopes of catching a glimpse of him. I remember my city editor, Ken Smart, calling me and asking me the size and mood of the crowd. I estimated the number and told him the crowd seemed to be more curious than angry.

I had expected to rest up on Sunday. After sleeping late, I remained in bed watching television. It was my first opportunity to watch television coverage of the assassination events. I was relaxed when about 11:20 a.m. NBC was showing the transfer of Oswald from the city jail.

Suddenly, a figure emerged from the crowd in the jail basement and shot Oswald. There was wild scuffling and the gunman yelled, "You know me, I'm Jack Ruby!"

The NBC newsman on the scene, Tom Pettit, standing only a few feet from Oswald, hardly missed a beat. "He's been shot - Lee Oswald has been shot! There is panic and pandemonium!" Pettit told the millions in his live television audience.

As for me, I almost levitated from the bed in pure astonishment.

In the jail basement, Jack Beers, a Dallas Morning News photographer, had triggered his camera as soon as Ruby leaped from the crowd with a gun. Beers took an excellent picture. But Bob Jackson of the Times Herald snapped his shutter a split-second later and got an even better one. In Jackson's shot, Oswald is grimacing as the bullet tears into his body. Bob won a Pulitzer Prize for his photograph.

Minutes after Oswald was shot my telephone rang, and it was Ken Smart summoning me back to work. Among other things, I gathered information about Jack Ruby, whom I did not know but had seen around the Times Herald building and the courthouse. Ruby, a nightclub owner, was one of those people who like to hang around newspaper offices, radio stations, police stations, courthouses and such places. The Dallas County sheriff, Bill Decker, knew Ruby well and told me of some of Ruby's relatively minor law violations. Ruby, for instance, had beaten up one of his striptease girls a few months earlier. That Sunday I also went to a sub-courthouse in Oak Cliff to dig up some complaints filed against Ruby. The sub-courthouse was closed but was opened just for me.

In the days, weeks, and months following that weekend, I wrote many stories dealing with the assassination and subsequent events. I remember, for instance, writing the first story in the Times Herald about the spontaneous outpouring of money sent to the widow of Officer Tippit. She eventually received more than $640,000 as Americans opened their hearts and their pocketbooks to her and her family. I also interviewed Marguerite Oswald, the accused assassin's mother, among others.

Jerry and I covered many of the legal hearings involving Jack Ruby. We heard Tom Howard, one of Ruby's earlier lawyers, loudly declare in the pressroom that "Jack Ruby shouldn't be tried for murder–instead he should get a Congressional Medal of Honor." Howard was reprimanded by the bar association for that statement and was dropped by the Ruby family. Jerry and I then got to know the flamboyant San Francisco lawyer, Melvin Belli, and his equally colorful partner, Joe Tonahill of Jasper, Texas. We already knew young Phil Burleson, Ruby's other trial lawyer, who has since made millions as a criminal lawyer.

The Times Herald had more than a half-dozen reporters covering the trial itself and tried to have two reporters in the courtroom at all times. When one reporter would leave the courtroom to call in, another would take his place. As I recall, I covered the running story only twice although I wrote many sidebars (related stories) from both within and outside the courtroom. Reporters filled up most of the space in the courtroom and I remember once sitting next to Eric Sevareid. Sometimes I would be covering other courthouse news while the trial was going on.

A long line would form each day as the public competed for the few remaining seats left in the courtroom. All sorts of people showed up in the line, including a legless woman who scooted around on roller skates. Several would-be spectators were carrying concealed revolvers and were hustled off as soon as they were found out.

One of the strangest things that happened outside the courtroom was an escape from the county jail upstairs. Five or six prisoners, as I recall, escaped. They ended up running down the hall outside the courtroom. Several television cameramen were in the hall but they were so startled they failed to film the escape. The jailbreak, of course, added to the flurry of bad national and international publicity Dallas attracted. "Oh, Dallas!" the New York Daily News sardonically bannered the story. When I called this story in, the city desk at first couldn't believe it and sent a young reporter, Darwin Payne, down to double-check on me.

Some reporters were trying to tout the Jack Ruby case as the "trial of the century," but it wasn't. There was no suspense because millions had seen Ruby shoot Oswald on television. Melvin Belli's defense was that Ruby was suffering "psychomotor epilepsy" and had a sort of mental seizure that caused him to have an "irresistible impulse" to shoot Oswald. In other words, as Flip Wilson might have put it, "the devil made him do it."

I worked for another seven years for the Times Herald and tried to keep up with all the various conspiracy rumors and theories, and over the past 20 years I have read and reviewed at least a half-dozen books about the assassination. Since joining the LSU journalism faculty in 1970, I have occasionally talked to classes and other groups about the assassination. Some people seem to think I should know "what really happened" simply because I was standing nearby at the time. I, of course, don't.

However, I have never been completely satisfied with the Warren Report conclusion that Lee Harvey Oswald, acting alone, was the assassin. Even Lyndon B. Johnson, shortly before his death, told Walter Cronkite he did not believe the commission, and he was the man who appointed it. Another reason I have looked askance at the Warren Report is that no one from the commission talked to me even though the commission printed Mrs. Hill's accusations against me. Besides, the Warren Report misspelled my name by adding an "e" to the end of it.

In my opinion, the two most knowledgeable Dallas reporters about the assassination were Jimmy Kerr, a veteran television and radio reporter, and Hugh Aynesworth, then with the Dallas Morning News and later with Newsweek magazine and the Times Herald. Jimmy told me, "We spent years looking into all those conspiracy rumors, and they would always fall through although we did find a lot of things that were exceedingly strange."

Facts and Photos

By Tom Alyea

Editor's Note:

Tom Alyea, the only newsman to join the initial police search team on the sixth floor of the Texas School Book Depository on November 22, 1963, denounces the disruption of the barricade fashioned of boxes as he first saw it.

Alyea, former WFAA newsman who recorded the panic on Dealey Plaza explains that the positioning of boxes was destroyed before the general press with still cameras were allowed in the building. He had completed his work in photographing everything of note and returned to his station long before the building was opened to the general press.

He recorded three cartridges where they landed after they were ejected from the rifle. He recorded the rifle as it was found, before it was touched. All such evidence is available to those who subscribe to his newsletter, JFK FACTS, mentioned later.

I was the first newsman into the building and the only newsman to accompany the search team as they went from floor to floor searching for the person who fired the shots. At this time, we did not know the president had been hit. I rushed in with a group of plain clothesmen and a few uniformed officers.

I turned to film the police rushing in the door behind me and saw Kent Biffle in my viewfinder as he passed in front of my lens. Kent was a first team byline reporter for the *Dallas Morning News*. I have seen this shot many times in the past thirty years as it is used in countless television reports on the assassination. One can count on seeing it on national television every November 22nd. Kent made it into the building only a second or two before a commanding voice yelled for the uniformed officers to close and lock the door. Today, Kent is a very popular columnist for the *Dallas Morning News*, and little do his readers realize when they see the close-up picture of Kent as he rushed into the Texas School Book Depository that this is the man who now writes the column they enjoy. Kent's young face will be preserved to the world and in the annals of journalism as testimony to his news alertness in responding to the opening seconds of an explosive news event.

I had a camera to my face and I doubt that he saw me. I then turned to follow the search team that was on its way to the rear elevator, to start the floor by floor search. We searched every floor, all the way to the roof. The gunman could have still been in the building. Finding nothing, they started back down. After approximately 18 minutes, they were joined by Captain Fritz, who had first gone to Parkland Hospital.

The barricade on the sixth floor ran parallel to the windows extending in an "L" shape that ended against the front wall between the first and second twin windows. The height of the stack of boxes was a minimum of 5 ft. I looked over the barricade and saw three shell casings laying on the floor in front of the second window in the two window casement. They were scattered in an area that could be covered by a bushel basket. They were located about half way between the inside of the barricade and the low brick wall under the windows. No shell casings were touching the wall or the inside of the barricade. I set my lens focus at the estimated distance from the camera to the floor and held the camera over the top of the barricade and filmed them before anybody went into the enclosure. I could not position my eye to the camera's view finder to get the shot. After filming the casings with my wide angle lens, from a height of 5 ft., I asked Captain Fritz, who was standing at my side, if I could go behind the barricade and get a close-up shot of the casings. He told me that it would be better if I got my shots from outside the barricade. He then rounded the pile of boxes and entered the enclosure. This was the first time anybody walked between the barricade and the windows.

Fritz then walked to the casings, picked them up and held them in his hand over the top of the boxes for me to get a close-up shot of the evidence. I filmed about eight seconds of a close-up shot of the shell casings in Captain Fritz's hand. I stopped filming, and thanked him. I do not recall if he placed them in his pocket or returned them back to the floor, because I was preoccupied with recording other views of the crime scene. I have been asked many times if I thought it was peculiar that the Captain of Homicide picked up evidence with his hands. Actually, that was the first thought that came to me when he did it, but I rationalized that he was the homicide expert and no prints could be taken from spent shell casings. Therefore, any photograph of shell casings taken after this, is staged and not correct. It is highly doubtful that the shell casings that appear in Dallas police photos of the crime scene are the same casings that were found originally. The originals by this time were probably in a plastic bag at police headquarters. Why? Probably this was a missing link in the report the police department had to send to the FBI and they had to stage it and the barricade box placement to complete their report and photo records.

The position of the barricade, while difficult to follow for one who was not there, is important because of the difference in photographs seen today.

There are about four different box positions.

1) There was one box in the barricade stack that was considerably higher than the others. This box is the one that can be seen in the photos taken from outside the window by Tom Dillard, because it was high enough to catch the sunlight and still be seen from the ground below. It is not to be confused with the second box set at an angle in the window sill, that was used as a brace for the assassin's rifle.

2) A portion of this box can also be seen in these same photos taken by Tom Dillard. It shows-up in the lower right hand corner of the picture.

3) Two boxes were stacked on the floor, inside the window, to give arm support to the assassin. The top box was one of the two boxes from which the crime lab lifted palm prints.

4) The fourth box of importance was on the floor behind the sniper location. Officers also lifted palm prints from this box. It is suspected that the sniper sat on this box while he waited for the motorcade to pass.

The positioning of boxes 2, 3, and 4 were recorded by the police crime lab. They are the only boxes involved in the crime scene.

The actual positioning of the barricade was never photographed by the police. Its actual positioning is only on my movie footage, which was taken before the police started dismantling the arrangement.

We all looked over the barricade to see the half open window with three boxes piled to form a shooting rest for a gunman. One box was actually on the window sill, tilted at an angle. There was a reason for this that I cover in my JFK Facts newsletter. The shooting location consists of two windows set together to form one single window. (The police photo showing the shell casings laying next to the brick wall was staged later by crime lab people who did not see the original positioning because they were not called upon the scene until after the rifle was found nearly an hour later.)

You will notice that I said: "I held my camera over the barricade to film the casings." This is because the height of the barricade that ran parallel to the windows extended in an "L" shape that ended against the front wall between the first and second twin windows. The height of the stack of boxes was a minimum of 5 ft. and I could not position my eye to the camera's view finder to get the shot.

Only recently I saw a picture of Lt. Day with a news still cameraman on the 6th floor. Day was shown pointing to the location where the rifle was found. This was nearly 3:30 or after. It was my understanding that Day and Studebaker had taken the prints, rifle and home-made sack back to police headquarters. I personally would like to know what they were doing back at the scene unless it was to reconstruct shots they had failed to take during the primary investigation. But this evidence had been destroyed and they were forced to create their own version. The photo I have seen of the barricade wasn't even close. I have also seen recently a police photo of the assassin's lair taken from a high angle which indicates that it was shot before the barricade box arrangement was destroyed, but it did not show the barricade itself. This has no bearing on the case other than the public has never seen the original placement. I show it in my JFK Facts newsletter.

Police officers who claim they were on the 6th floor when the assassin's window was found have reported that they saw chicken bones at or near the site. One officer reported that he saw chicken bones on the floor near the location. Another said he saw chicken bones on the barricade boxes, while another reported that he saw chicken bones on the box which was laying across the window sill. Some of these officers have given testimony as to the location and positioning of the shell casings. Their testimony differs and none of it is true. I have no idea why they are clinging to these statements. They must have a reason. Perhaps it is because they put it in a report and they must stick to it.

One officer stated that he found the assassin's location at the 6th floor window. He went on to say that as he and his fellow officers were leaving the building, he passed Captain Fritz coming in. He said he stopped briefly to tell Captain Fritz that he had found the assassin's lair at the 6th floor window. This seems highly unlikely because Captain Fritz joined us on the 5th floor and aided in the search. The chances are great that this, or these officers heard the report, that stemmed from WFAA-TV's incorrect announcement that the chicken bones were found on the 6th floor. This officer or officers perhaps used this information to formulate their presence at the scene. There were no chicken bones found on the 6th floor. We covered every inch of it and I filmed everything that could possibly be suspected as evidence. There definitely were no chicken bones on or near the barricade or boxes at the window. I shot close-up shots of this entire area. The most outstanding puzzle as to why these officers are sticking to this story is the fact they claim to have found the sniper's location, then left the building, as they said to join the investigators at the Tippit shooting location. I have never seen a report that indicates they attempted to use any telephone in the building in an attempt to notify other investigators. They just left the scene to check another assignment, and by chance ran into Capt. Fritz coming in the front door. They claim to have placed a detective at the location but they did not relay their finding to any other officer before they left the building. I presume that the alleged detective that allegedly left at the scene was instructed to stand there until someone else stumbled upon the scene, or they found time to report it after investigating the Tippit scene. Sorry, it doesn't wash.

I do however know that Officer Mooney was present when the rifle was found because I took film of him at the scene. He is shown talking to another detective, but this was nearly an hour after the sniper's location was found at the window. I have no idea when he arrived. We ended up with more men that when we started. As they joined us during the search the latecomers would bring us the latest news of the president's condition. When Captain Fritz arrived 18 minutes after we started, he brought news that both Governor Connally and the president had been hit but by the time he left, the seriousness of their wounds was unknown. Fritz left the hospital almost immediately when he was notified that a search was underway in the Texas School Book Depository for the sniper. We in the search team had no phones, radios or TV sets. As I recall, we learned that the president was dead about the time we found the rifle. I don't know who brought us this word. Several officers arrived while we were waiting for Lt. Day. One of them was Roger Craig who is responsible for giving much misinformation to the press. None of us were prepared to hear that the president's wound was a fatal one. We thought perhaps it was a minor thing or possibly a flesh wound. It was a stunning shock, and our attitude of the rifle had suddenly changed. We stared at the small portion of the butt as it lay under the overhang boxes while we waited for Lt. Day to arrive and recover the weapon that killed our president. I give an account of this in JFK Facts.

Now, back to finding the assassin's window.

When we arrived on the 6th floor and the location was found, there were no detectives or officers at the location. Captain Fritz ordered three uniformed officers to stand guard and see that nothing was touched until it was secured. (I have a photograph of these uniformed policemen standing guard. I made it from a frame in my movie film.) We finished combing the 6th floor, looking for the assassin or any other evidence. Finding nothing more at this time Captain Fritz ordered all of us to the elevator and we started searching the 7th floor and from there we went to the roof.

Nothing in the way of evidence was found so we retraced our search back down, floor by floor. Shortly after we arrived back on the 6th floor, Deputy Eugene Boone located the assassin's rifle almost completely hidden by some overhanging boxes near the stairwell. I filmed it as it was found. In my shot, the figure of Captain Fritz is standing within the enclosure next to the rifle. He knew then that the possibility of a fire fight with the sniper had greatly diminished. He dispatched one of his men to go down and call for the crime lab. About fifteen minutes later, Lt. Day and Studebaker arrived. Still pictures were taken of the positioning of the rifle, then Lt. Day slid it out from it's hiding place and held it up for all of us to see. The world has seen my shot of this many times. Lt. Day immediately turned toward the window behind him and started dusting the weapon for fingerprints. Day was still within the enclosure formed by the surrounding boxes. I filmed him lifting prints from the rifle. He lifted them off with scotch tape and placed them on little white cards. When he had finished, he handed the rifle to Captain Fritz. Fritz pulled the bolt back and a live round ejected and landed on the boxes below. Fritz put the cartridge in his pocket. I did not see Fritz pick up anything other than the live round. If a clip was ejected, I didn't notice it, nor did I see Fritz pick up a second object. I have learned that the six round clip for this rifle ejects when the last round is injected into the chamber. If this is the case, there must have been three rounds in the rifle when it was found. Fritz ejected one... another went into the chamber when the bolt was closed and one still remained in the clip. I have no idea whether the police made a notation of this, or if the rounds were dusted for fingerprints.

After filming Lt. Day and Captain Fritz with the rifle, I moved across the room to Crime Lab Detective Studebaker, who was busy at the assassin's window dusting for fingerprints. Apparently Studebaker had finished taking pictures of the window box arrangement because over half of the barricade had been torn down. An of the boxes that joined the principle barricade to the wall had been removed. This would provide the photographer an easy shot of the window, without having to stand on another pile of boxes to shoot over the barricade. Before the boxes were removed, the assassin's window could not be seen by anyone standing on the floor, unless they were only a few inches from the pile of boxes so they could see over them.

I filmed Captain Fritz talking with associates in this dismantled area, along with Studebaker, who was dusting the Dr. Pepper bottle which had been brought up to him from the 5th floor. This is all recorded on my film. I never learned if prints were lifted from the pop bottle. I'm not sure if anybody ever asked.

I took the film from my camera, placed it back into its metal can, wrapped the tape around it, and tossed it to our News Editor A. J. L'Hoste, who was waiting outside with the other newsmen who were not allowed in the building. A. J. raced it to the television station which was about three blocks away. About fifteen minutes later the world saw the murder weapon, where it was found and pictures of the crime lab people dusting it for finger prints, and the shell casings that once housed those bullets. They also saw how the assassin prepared for his ambush and the view he had of the killing zone.

PART II
☎
THE REPORTERS

The gallery in which the reporters sit has become the Fourth Estate of the realm.

Thomas Babington Macauley
English historian, essayist, statesman
(1800-1859)

Our Liberty depends on the freedom of the press, and that cannot be limited without being lost.

Thomas Jefferson
3rd President of the United States
(1743-1826)

Please realize that the first duty of newspaper men is to get the news and PRINT THE NEWS.

William Randolph Hearst
American press lord
(1863-1951)

Seven

Reminiscences of the Herald Crew

There were about 35 reporters assigned to "cityside" in 1963, then city editor Kenneth Smart estimates. We never thought it was enough. But now, facing it without bias, I must say that we worked hard, but we had our fun, too. We saw to it that we attended every press party, and many spent their lunch hours at the Press Club. I remember an Associated Press staff member, a good looking blonde, who was usually on a diet, although she didn't seem to need it. Anyway, she sometimes drank her lunch in the form of martinis at the Press Club. She returned chirruping gleefully on the arms of AP reporters.

Jim Featherston remembers that he and his pals didn't need much of an excuse to go have a beer in late morning, And there were other forms of pleasure. If you had your work done, the Herald didn't care what you were writing. Jim Lehrer, co-host of the PBS television MacNeil-Lehrer Hour, was then a reporter. Many afternoons, after completing his assignments, he typed away at his first book, *Viva Max*. It sold very well, and made a fine movie, suitable for families. I knew when he was working on his book because he chuckled as he wrote. Now, along with television duties, he regularly publishes a series of books.

MacNeill was never part of the Herald crew, but after the assassination, a few of us heard that he was in Dallas covering the assassination. When some left the press cars at the crime scene, MacNeill ran up the steps of the Texas School Book Depository, seeking a telephone. The story was that he met Lee Oswald leaving the building, and asked where he could find a telephone. Oswald gave him directions. What a story "that got away".

Jim Lehrer was on the federal beat, and usually present in Dallas. Bob Hollingsworth was our Washington correspondent, and seldom present. He was in Dallas on November 22.

My first assignment was the obituary beat–the lowest of the low. The "obit" writer before me was charismatic young Jim Koethe. Jim was one of the most talented reporters I would ever meet.

Koethe was also the best feature writer I ever read. I have always described to interested reporters what I believe was the best feature "lede" ever written. After being prodded or allowed to try gliding, Jim wrote a story which began with the following two sentences:

> "A chicken flew over Dallas Wednesday.
> Me."

The remainder of the story described the actual event.

Bill Sloan, in his book *Breaking the Silence*, relayed a quote made by Dan Martin: "Koethe was a good writer. He was so good that he was able to run at about half-speed most of the time and get away with it." I learned from Jim and other talented reporters and editors.

As the departing obit writer, Koethe was obliged to "show me the ropes", and then he could move on to general assignments. Training by Koethe consisted of one day's intensive instruction, and then he swiftly deserted me. I faced him down at a party one night and said that I damn well knew his training was so detailed and intense only so he would never have to man the desk again. He agreed.

Jim's death was the first of our crew attributed by some to the assassination. He had been allowed to view Ruby's apartment the night Oswald was killed. Also present was Bill Hunter, a reporter from California. Jim was killed by a karate chop in September, 1964. Hunter was shot to death in a police department in Long Beach, California, in April of that year. Hunter's death was first ruled an accident but eventually changed to "improper handling of a firearm by the officers involved". The officers served probation.

I was a quick study because clumsy stories or obvious errors embarrassed me beyond endurance. I was promoted to an editor/reporter's slot within six months.

No one wants to start the day at seven a.m. asking who died the night before, especially a young widow. And our "contacts" at the mortuaries, while indispensable, made sure that a new obit writer passed their "regulations" before trust was established. I remember them describing an elderly woman who had "come in" the night before. At least they thought it was a woman, my contact concluded with a laugh. They were "good ole boys" and we were not allowed the luxury of taking offense.

Instead, my hatred of the beat arose from having to talk to a widow before she had time, sometimes even minutes, to compose herself. Or talking to parents who had lost a child. Often they would arrive in the newsroom a few hours later, lovingly carrying a framed portrait of the child. In those days, each obit was written by me, and checked out for accuracy both with the funeral home and the family. Almost as difficult were obits where the deceased had been married several times and each set of relatives claimed to be first of kin.

After the obits had "gone to bed" by noon, I had other assignments in the afternoon. At first I wrote features about 100 year old women–few and far between in those days–holidays, and covered every damn parade that came down Main Street. Later I graduated to a few hard news stories and features on visiting celebrities.

We reporters were a close group and depended on each other for support and to fill in the gaps in our storehouse of knowledge. Stewart Doss, a crusty middle-aged widower, sat to my right, and became my mentor. He was one of the best. Stewart's style was totally different than Koethe's. He made religion news, which it actually was, by revealing the business side, the turfish side, and the personal side. He taught me to never write about a subject without calling and interviewing at least three of the subject's friends.

Blackie Sherrod, who helped on the Presidential desk, still writes. He is now employed by the *Dallas Morning News*, and I have seen his stories in other newspapers. There were Herald reporters who went onto higher status in the field, such as Seth Kantor and Bill Sloan, writers of several books, and, of course, Jim Lehrer. Another local reporter was Hugh Aynesworth, who closely followed the assassination story. He still resides in Dallas but declined to respond to telephone messages I left on his answering machine. He knew Marina well, and now that she is interested in discovering the truth, perhaps Aynesworth will reconsider his silence.

Reporters and editors I remember well included Ben Stevens, Bill Fenley, Tom LePere, Charlie Damron, Tom Ayres, Dean Singleton, Richard Curry, business editor, John Schollkopf, Keith Shelton, photographer Bob Jackson and medical writer Bill Burris. But, I too must admit that others are only dim memories. I would need a school yearbook to place them. There are concrete memories as well.

Each reporter had an oversized wire mesh wastebaskets beside his desk, which we quickly filled with wadded up first drafts and "puff" (press releases) which were routed to us. Stewart Doss chain smoked, as most of us did...part of the lifestyle. One day he set his wastebasket on fire. There was little interest from others as he thumped one leg into the flames until they disappeared, leaving a trail of black smoke. Doss went back to writing and ignored the smoldering mess. Stewart was a recovering alcoholic, and did not join the rest of us as we drank Scotch whiskey and traveled from one press party to another. Liking Scotch was another requirement for acceptance. For me, it was an acquired taste, not unpleasant. Some claimed they depended on the cocktail parties for their evening meal. With three young children waiting at home with a patient, but rational housekeeper, I was slightly better grounded than some.

A photographer who reluctantly stepped into fame became a working friend. Bob Jackson won a Pulitzer Prize for his photo of Ruby firing a slug into the stomach of Lee Oswald. His camera lens caught Oswald's face contorted in acute pain as the broad back of Jack Ruby lunged toward him. Bob and I were paired by my choice. The Herald had its drawbacks. Printed on inferior newsprint, photographs lacked the impact of those published in the *Dallas Morning News*. Although another photographer on staff was the favorite of the Women's Editor Vivian Castleberry because of his artistry, I sought and usually received Bob's services. He flooded homes with light and the furnishings burst from the dull newsprint. At the Press Club, Morning News reporters chided us–"you have to be from the Herald, you wear it all over you." Bob and I ignored it all, and dashed from tasteful mansions to ostentatious homes in his Porsche.

The link between Bob and me was our shared enthusiasm for our work and the fact that we both had young families. It ventured into warm friendship on my part. When he was the first pressman to spot a rifle being pulled back into the sixth floor of the Texas School Book Depository, I never doubted what he had seen. Monday morning after the assassination, he developed his film taken in the basement of the police station the day before. I purposely hung around until he jubilantly shouted from the darkroom–"I got it". Jostled by the surging crowd the moment before the shot, Bob feared he had been a mili-second too late for the perfect photograph. Typically, the Morning News gave more front page space to Jack Beers' photo than the Herald afforded Bob's historic prize winner. The Herald was likened by many to a "cheapskate"–unwilling to spend money on its reporters or newsprint to be the leader it might have been. But I have no experience in publishing costs, and cannot be a fair judge.

The setting in the newsroom was vastly different from the newsrooms of today, with computers and "desktop" publishing, but no different than others in the sixties.

In 1963, the composing room was one floor below. I spent my share of time leaning over trays of lead letters which composing men deftly handled in wide spread hands. The reporter or editor had to read upside down and backwards. The composers had the advantage; they only read backwards. Getting along with these men was essential. They could and did make or break you. Raise their ire, and your story might end in the middle of a sentence, or contain spelling you never imagined.

I recall a union negotiation between the press and composing men and the Herald. (Reporters were not union members.) An editor reading a page one proof "on deadline" jumped a foot and screamed "stop the presses" as he reached a wire story from England. Princess Margaret, who was pregnant at the time, had canceled her "pubic engagements". The editor's sharp eye changed the word to "public" as intended. Such "oversights" were less common when relations were going smoothly.

Only once did I have the opportunity to "stop the presses". We used the exact words; equivocating would not get results. I was editing the Sunday women's section near midnight on Saturday night–a rotating shift we all dreaded. As the "proof" of the front page of the women's section with color photo, plunked down the tube, I quickly discovered there was no cutline beneath the picture of the society ladies. Their beaming faces stared out of a third-of-a-page photo, totally unidentified. When I phoned the order downstairs, there was brief hesitation (I was, after all, only a woman). But for that instant, my word was law. I took the stairs to the composing room at a run. A composer found the cutline and swiftly rebuilt the page. Vivian said I did the right thing. We knew which side our bread was buttered on.

"Cityside", I have reported, was largely a man's world. I was the only woman there during my time as an obituary writer. Later, I believe there was a female education writer, the others were all men. In actuality, I always enjoyed working for men more than women. I don't believe I was prejudiced against female supervisors. Men got to the point more quickly in my opinion, and I responded to them more comfortably. Tom LePere, the assistant city editor, and a great teacher for me, if only by his corrections. Tom and I were contemporaries. I was older than most beginning reporters. The other editors on the desk taught me the craft of reporting. Sometimes by brief lectures; more often by letting me learn by my mistakes. Stewart Doss was the only man who actually explained points of reporting, such as the unwritten rule that the lede paragraph should not contain more than thirty words. That rule necessitated referring to the subject by description in the lede, then using full titles in succeeding paragraphs. I still consider "writing" an art–"reporting" a craft.

After I became Home Editor, I enjoyed a few perks–a trip to the furniture market at Chicago, a number of banquets, and buying furniture wholesale. I have none of the furniture left. Raising three children who used it daily, as well as normal aging, led to its demise. But I was more content for a practical reason. On the women's side I worked, for the most part, a Monday through Friday week, which caused this single mother less guilt. But I emphasize that in later years, I served stints as police and city hall reporter in smaller towns, paying my dues. So much so that during my present marriage I returned to Dallas but worked only a few months as editor of the suburgan section of a smaller daily. Time with my husband was infrequent as I covered weekly city council meetings and every small town election a burg could have. After a total of nine years, I left the news world...regretfully.

Like many ex-reporters, I entered the world of public relations, and ultimately non-profit corporate management. But I still can hear the roar of the giant presses and miss the excitement of the print news world.

Eight

Reporters Are People, Too

During the years, I have talked to many reporters and editors about the stereotyped reporter. In stereotype, the print reporter is a shy person with an inquisitive mind. I once talked to an experienced reporter who admitted that when she covered her first assignment, she walked around the block three times before getting the nerve to knock on the door and begin her first interview.

Then why are they such by-line hogs? It's simple–some one is reading your story and either admiring or hating you for it, and you haven't shown your face. I am not speaking of television "reporters". They are another breed altogether. The print reporter usually shrinks when he has made an error. Few reporters ridicule each other, because they dread committing errors themselves. They want to write an accurate story, but there is always a time when the inevitable error occurs. The daily deadline contributes to mistakes, but has allure as well. When the day is over, its news is dead. Every new day holds the possibility of excitement and new opportunities. A reporter's nervousness is usually hidden behind an aggressive attitude that melts away in the reporter's private life.

One day a very independent female reporter's chair went over backward and she landed awkwardly on her back. Male reporters across the aisle automatically rushed to her aid. Her shout could have been heard in Fort Worth–"DON'T TOUCH ME." No one laughed. Typing resumed. The mishap hadn't happened. Another lost a heel to her shoe–probably two inches high. With a crowded schedule, she apparently didn't have time to have it repaired. I still see her walking sedately around the newsroom, one foot on the floor the other tilted upward to make her gait level.

Some of the crew were valiant. One had cancer and worked up until her last three days of life. Although she was fondly remembered, there were no comments on her choice to work until the bitter end. Another suffered from rheumatoid arthritis. I learned from an editor, not from her, that it took her over an hour to dress in the mornings. She never complained. We usually didn't share our troubles. We were a strange, private lot.

But some were always ready to party. I had my share of wildness, not totally because I was a reporter. Before my first marriage, I had been a "good girl" and never sowed any wild oats. I think most mature people have sampled a little of the spice of life. At one party, a male reporter and I had too much to drink and decided to leave and go to his apartment. Our cars were in a multi-story parking garage. We left my car there, intending to return for it after our escapade. Unfortunately, it didn't work out that way. Once in his apartment, disrobing amid his under garments strewn about, I began to grow sober. Down to my slip, bra, panties, "garter belt" and nylons, I decided the entire "affair" had been a mistake. I saw no graceful way to discuss the matter. I panicked, grabbed his car keys from the dresser and my dress. Pulling the dress over my head, I ran to his car. I started the car, drove home and went to bed. In the morning–plagued by guilt and a giant-sized hangover, I drove to the garage, parked his car, got into my own and went to work.

He was already working. I telephoned across the twenty open feet, told him where his car was, and apologized. He only said, "Okay". Naturally, there was no second date.

I never wrote for the entertainment section, but I haunted it, usually searching for free opera tickets. I also reviewed books, as did several others. When free first editions arrived, they were passed on to persons with interest in the subject matter, and we became critics. It was a heady feeling. We became over night experts, and wore our crowns slightly askew.

Since we saw each other every day, newsroom romances abounded. Two reporters married and we gossiped about whether they were "right" for each other. It didn't occur to us that it was none of our business and we were not entitled to speculate. One night I went to dinner with a female reporter and her husband; proving that I had a respectable side. We maintained a cooperative attitude toward each other, even if we didn't get along. There were fewer cliques than at most places I have worked.

We each had our professional style, and I won't pretend that it was always pleasant for the interviewee. In the 1960's it was not acceptable to disagree with a person we were interviewing, unless it could be done in a flattering manner. That was seldom possible. When I interviewed "Dearie" Cabell, the wife of Mayor Earle Cabell, the published story detailed not a single fault or regret in her life. She sent me a lace handkerchief in appreciation. When today's audiences complain of a television personality's saccharine style, as some do about Barbara Walters, I think they should have been around us. Politeness was the unwritten order.

Not that we were captive to writing reams of lies or obviously self-serving material about a subject. We had our own ways to defeat distasteful stories. Often the stories were written quite briefly, therefore withholding undue publicity. And we had various ways to trip up the subject who was untruthful. I had my own method, made possible because I took shorthand. My past years as a legal secretary served me well. I had taken depositions in shorthand (and hated it) so my notes were more detailed than those of some reporters. My notes could be very close to the accuracy achieved today by use of a tape recorder. Few citizens realized that we did a lot of covering up for them–correcting bad grammar, not mentioning the slip dipping below the dress, etc. If I felt the unsavory subject deserved it, I took explicit notes and wrote exactly what he said, down to every "uh", "I seen..", "everybody knows he's that-a-way..."

Such memories help me emphasize that we didn't play pranks or make fun of each other. When I first became Home Editor I wrote an eight inch piece of puff about a new product, "Teflon". Throughout the story, I typed "Telfon". When I saw the story in print, I "died a thousand deaths". Naturally, the only person who commented on the error was my mother. Reporters were far easier to please.

A later venture, in 1964 and 65, separated the men from the boys. Some of us thought that, as a group, we were underpaid. The pressmen were members of a union, and their pay was reportedly higher than ours. So we foolishly tried to organize as local unit of the Newspaper Guild of the AFL-CIO. It had been tried once before and several "agitators" were fired. The Guild sent an organizer to work with us, which didn't particularly excite him. The Herald was regarded as a looser. They had worked with the reporters in an earlier attempt to organize and it failed badly. The only other southwestern paper to have a union for reporters was in San Antonio. And that union was reportedly weak. We formed a 13-member steering committee. I was the only woman. We met in hotel rooms and argued, planned and counted those we were to convince. Jim Lehrer was among us, but I don't believe his heart was in it. Just as things seemed to be going well, I received a death threat relayed to me by a sympathetic reporter on another newspaper. I didn't give it a second thought, and went on working. The organizer had emphasized that we must do our jobs even better than usual as we organized. And we really tried not to discuss the issue at work. It was impossible, however, as others approached us. Our need to convince them made it difficult to cut short the conversation. Truthfully, most of the lobbying took place after hours. I honestly felt we had a right to organize, being the daughter of a union man. The publisher obviously disagreed.

By the day of the secret vote, we knew we were whipped, but not how badly. Keith Shelton answered a question posed by me recently. He heard we lost mainly by "no" votes from sports and the women's section. Sports reporters because they didn't need it and women because they were afraid that if higher pay was given, the Herald would find better female reporters! I'm glad I didn't hear the latter.

We had a post-election party, at Lehrer's home, if I remember correctly. I sat on the floor and got drunk, eventually sobbing in humiliation at our poor showing. My information is that management bought off pivotal reporters with small raises or their own columns. Reporters were column-crazy. I had my own, so I was active on principle and couldn't have been bought off. I even thought I was adequately paid because I received $5 more a week than some reporters because I was a "head of household".

Someone at the post-election party probably decided I was suicidal, so they sent an outside photographer home with me. Once in my own home, my ire and embarrassment gave way to a desperate need for sleep. But as I grew quieter, he got drunker. Finally, I had to call for help to get him home. There were even worse exhibitions. The day after the election I went to work ashamed and depressed. I wasn't the only one. A reporter–male–had worked most of the night, drinking beer all the while. He was found by the early staff sitting at his desk in his under shirt and boxer shorts with empty beer cans around.

He was taken home and given several days to recover.

It was seldom dull at the *Dallas Times Herald*–we didn't believe in dullness.

Nine

Aborted Investigation

The reporters, at least two from the *Dallas Times Herald*, did begin an investigation. On Monday, I stood by for several minutes as Jim Koethe and another interested journalist began their own investigation with semi-seriousness. There is no way to know if they had a fully outlined plan; probably not, since they obviously had no official assignment. Chief Curry wasn't talking, so understandably they began where they had left off Sunday afternoon–when Koethe and others had visited Jack Ruby's apartment.

Jim Featherston says that he and Koethe finished off Friday night sharing drinks and talking over the similarities in the assassinations of Presidents Lincoln and Kennedy and events of the day.

Years later, Bill Sloan wrote, in his book *JFK: Breaking the Silence*, that on Sunday afternoon Jim, in the press room at city hall, was hailed by Bill Hunter, a "close friend while both were reporters at the Wichita Falls Record". Sloan also should be credited for explaining that Koethe was pronounced "Koty".

Hunter was in the Dallas press room Sunday for the same reason as Koethe, they were still working on the big story. According to Sloan, they went to the TV Bar. There Koethe saw three lawyers, C.A. Droby, Jim Martin and Tom Howard, who had done legal work for Jack Ruby in the past. The lawyers were sitting together with an out of town writer. Not to be outdone, Koethe led Hunter to join the group. They were waiting for Ruby's roommate, George Senator. Senator, Sloan wrote, joined them about 8 p.m., and eventually one of the writers decided he wanted a picture of Ruby. Koethe and Hunter followed the others to Ruby's apartment.

There the group "roamed freely about the apartment", but found nothing of interest. Droby told Sloan that Koethe made some notes, but remarked that "It was just a dumpy apartment".

Sloan reports that included in lengthy news coverage of Oswald's slaying and Ruby's arrest, was a paragraph saying that Droby was one of several lawyers who called at headquarters to consult with Ruby. Soon, his wife received two phone calls threatening the Drobys. She was warned twice that "they would be next" if her husband represented Ruby.

Monday Koethe and another reporter quickly began seeking an answer to a most intriguing part of the plot. Did Oswald know Jack Ruby? It was, after all, a continuation of what Koethe had begun the day before. It is quite possible that at least one had seen the same newsreel I had, and noticed the gleam of recognition on Oswald's face when he saw Ruby just before the bullet ripped into his gut.

There was the uncontroverted fact that if Oswald had walked southeast from his Beckley Street rooming house, he was headed in the direction of Jack Ruby's apartment. Investigating this possibility that there was a connection between Ruby and Oswald became quite innocently their first step. They were mapping his steps from the TSBD toward the Ruby apartment. Most likely, that day they had little doubt that Lee Oswald killed Officer J.D. Tippit. But these were not gullible guys. I believe the question would have arisen later.

If Koethe had been allowed to proceed with an investigation, he would also have fulfilled every direct assignment given him by the city desk. It seemed clear to me as I stood and watched them, that at least a series would come of their efforts.

Bearing explanation is the difference in investigative reporting in the 1960's and recent years, most notable in the Woodward and Bernstein coverage of Watergate. Once the *Washington Post* was supporting the W&B stories, the pair was allowed to work as a team. Their stories probably had high priority as the complicated story unfolded.

In the 60's, investigative reporting was usually done in "series", the kickoff hitting the Sunday paper with its large circulation and concluding Thursday or Friday. The stories had to be presented as a package to the editors before publication. There were two reasons. First, to determine if the writing met the editors' standards, and then close scrutiny was given for any content which might offend a major advertiser or public figure. An example is the series covering Dallas homicides written by Ben Stevens and Bob Vetito, which won first place in the 1965 Headliners Awards. I was first place winner the same year for a women's series. The same segregation of sex and content (women's section and "cityside") was exercised in submitting stories for possible awards as existed in the structure of the newsroom. As for content, my series was about sub-standard child care centers, a valid concern in those years.

There is no doubt in my mind that Jim Koethe was ready to look into the assassination story further. Was Oswald walking toward Ruby's apartment to receive a payoff to get out of town? Seth Kantor, Koethe and I, and surely thousands of others, thought, at that time that it might be the case. In fact, there was no other obvious reason for him to be walking in a southeasterly direction, except to receive money and other assistance. Applying common sense, or the law of probability, he was needing to hide out, get out of town, or simply kill some time.

At that time, Koethe was simply a general assignments reporter. Quickly, he received other unrelated assignments and not unlike Tom Alyea was sent an unwritten message. Get back to work.

By spring, 1964, Koethe received what, I agree with Sloan, was a plum assignment. He was promoted to full-time feature writer on the Herald's Sunday magazine section. It should be remembered there is more than one way to neutralize a trouble-maker. Remove him or promote him. Same result.

Details of the weekend before September 21, 1964 are best described by author Bill Sloan in *Breaking the Silence*. He wrote that an assistant city editor called Herald political writer Keith Shelton, who was still at home, and asked if he knew where Koethe was. He did not. Eventually an entry of Koethe's apartment by apartment complex personnel revealed the reporter lying dead, wrapped in a blanket. Personal items were missing. His car was later found several blocks away.

I remember the week of Koethe's death. I was shocked, and whispers began when the family avoided the memorial service we expected, and Jim literally "disappeared from the face of the earth".

Koethe's closest friend at the Herald, again according to Sloan, was Ben Stevens. They talked enough of the assassination that Ben felt sure Koethe knew nothing more than has been described here. However, Stephens and other friends of Koethe believed that the police and the DA were deliberately dragging their heels on the investigation of Koethe's death. According to Sloan, Stephens discovered that some of the DA's people believed it was a "queer deal" and that they were bowing from pressure of Koethe's relatives to drop the case. There was a suspect named Larry Dale Reno, whom they had discovered had one of Koethe's guns.

My memory is slightly different, so I suggest those who are interested read Sloan's book, if they haven't already. I was an innocent in the ways of homosexuality and heard the week of Jim's death that he may have died of strangulation, the sign of a homosexual encounter gone sour. Being the news-hen, as well as having liked Koethe and not believing he was homosexual, I asked a psychiatrist-friend about the practice and was frankly educated.

It was true that Koethe seemed to have no lasting relationships with women and bar hopped with or without his reporter friends. What he did on his own is speculative. However, in 1963, "star reporters" would not openly have homosexual relations. I did hear that Koethe's family wanted the matter quiet and private, and it was handled that way.

Sloan reported that there was "solid evidence that Koethe had just stepped out the shower when he surprised an intruder in his apartment". Jim Featherston, Keith Shelton and others did not believe he was homosexual. At my current age and understanding, it does not matter.

What does matter is that the shine of this reporter's talent was tarnished in those years. Now, perhaps we can, in a small way, restore it. Whether Jim Koethe had an outside life due to sexual preference, or because he had other friends, cannot be determined. I believe that he was still asking questions about the assassination, and, furthermore, what Koethe wanted to do, he did. He was unstoppable, except in one way. By death.

As for his death, and the subsequent stories about his sexual life, they did exactly what they were designed to do. They covered up anything of worth Jim Koethe might have doggedly turned up on the case. Koethe was quite possibly a victim twice over. Once, he was the innocent victim of a killer, and then again, he was the victim of unwarranted character assassination.

Any work of value on the assassination by Jim went to his grave with him. This is not an attempt to elevate Jim Koethe to sainthood. But if I had assembled an investigative team, I would have wanted him on it.

Stories related to the assassination were reported in the *Dallas Times Herald*. Some were scattered slices of life, some were unsolicited stories. Many proved false. There was no continuity among the published articles.

This is not to say that all or even most of the reporters believed that a conspiracy had transpired.

In fact, most did not give it much thought, leaving the work to the Warren Commission. I distinctly remember the elevation in status of those who "went to Washington" to testify.

Keith Shelton, a specialist in politics, believed most of the report. When I wrote to Jim Lehrer once, he seemed disinterested in contacting the reporters at the Herald. Tom Alyea, quoted herein, is sure in his mind that Lee Harvey Oswald was the lone assassin. Jim Koethe was at least intrigued by the possibility of unknown facts.

I believed in a conspiracy because of my own experience of a cover-up, and from my own particular brand of logic. Jim Featherston said in a recent letter that he encouraged his students at Louisiana State University to read on their own because it seemed that "there was something there". Seth Kantor admitted that it was hardly politically correct for him to pursue his independent investigation when he was at work in Washington covering the Johnson administration. He waited years before he explored the *Ruby Cover-Up.*

Much available information was unexplored, especially in Dallas. The cover-up became a "clamp-down".

I grew so impatient that I eventually wrote the Warren Commission and offered information about my talk with the physicians and the printed story. With a form letter, the Commission assured me that the matter had been covered. I threw the letter away.

When The Warren Commission Report was published, a fellow reporter offered to let me borrow his copy. I read several chapters, then stopped and returned the book. In the style of Harold Weisberg, I thought it was "hog wash".

I became discouraged, although I never ceased voicing doubts. By 1968, I was in Washington serving as press secretary to U.S. Representative Abraham Kazen, Democratic Congressman from Laredo, Texas. I received a mild tongue lashing from his staff simply because I spent a Saturday covering the Poor People's march on Washington. After I was given the opportunity to visit the White House newsroom, I realized that however low a level I occupied, I was in politics, and represented the Congressman. Later, as Managing Editor of *The Corpsman*, national newspaper for the Job Corps, I used my contacts to take my mother through the FBI training quarters. We were met by a public relations man who recited my dossier in brief before we began the tour. I regarded it then as an inferior publicity stunt, but later wondered if it carried a message.

A decade later, working for the State of Oklahoma, I was on Governor Dewey Bartlett's "radical list". I know this because my boss told me he had heard from the governor, directly or indirectly, questioning the advisability of hiring me. Fortunately for me, I was hired as a Public Information Officer. I could classify myself as one of those who may have benefited or been rewarded for doing nothing upsetting to the administration, although I cannot be certain. Certainly when I went to Washington, I had no trouble landing the very job I would have chosen. But if I could have traded the Washington experience with writing worthy news about the assassination, I would have made that choice.

I was interested, I knew there was a cover-up, and I found the conclusions of the Warren Commission ludicrous.

PART III
📖
DOCUFICTION
DATELINE DALLAS

...the states of virtue by which the soul possesses truth by way of affirmation or denial are five in number, i.e., art, scientific knowledge, practical wisdom, philosophic wisdom, intuitive reason; we do not include judgment and opinion because in those we may be mistaken.

Aristotle
Greek philosopher
(384-322)

Ten

Fiction Based on Fact vs. Evidence Built on Speculation

The cover-up of facts in the John F. Kennedy assassination was itself covered up for many years. When certain information could no longer be hidden, the excuse given was that early facts had been withheld in the interest of national security.

For the sake of belated frankness, it ought to be admitted that it was not in the interest of the American image to reveal that our country, like others, used "dirty tricks" to built up our status in world affairs. Allen Dulles in his book, *Craft of Intelligence*, would, by implication, have the reader believe that scurrilous behavior is committed only by foreign governments. Few U.S. citizens today are so naive as to believe in the moral purity of American intelligence. Release of information which could have brought about military action between the Soviets and the United States arguably should not have been released to the general public. However, to cover up facts that were only politically embarrassing to the United States is, in my opinion, a "dirty trick". Few Americans expect our government to be infallible.

J. Edgar Hoover certainly participated in the cover-up and even engineered many of its techniques. Should he have been allowed to make certain that American citizens believed that one lone man, in a psychotic condition, killed the President? What was his motive in blocking an investigation which could have discovered more than one murderer? There were, and still are suggestions that the assassination was "a local affair", committed by right wing Dallasites. If that had been correct, or even probative, Hoover could have garnered great honor by rounding up the most-wanted murderers of the century and sending them to their death in the American tradition. Instead he,

President Lyndon Johnson, and ultimately the entire Commission did, in my opinion, further the cover-up. There can be no other reason for such actions–in my belief–than that persons in highest authority had to cover up "things" which could not be revealed without great embarrassment to the government. If it was not within the government, the "cancer" referred to by President Johnson could have been cut away and dissected to benefit the country. Since such a course was not followed (and there were subsequent international cover-ups) many Americans believe, or speculate, that a conspiracy or conspiracies existed. I submit that those of us who do so believe, are without blame.

Hoover was not the only cover-up operative. Others, equally effective on a local level, were Dallas leaders and Dallas police. Some were primarily interested in the image of Dallas–first and always. Many were not instigators, because they were not "in the loop". Instead they simply had their jobs to do. However unwittingly, they spread the dark cloak further over the city. At times it is difficult to separate authentic Top Secret stamps from fakes. After the release of some information under the Freedom of Information Act, it became evident that prior withholding was done to conceal the actions of persons in high positions.

It was common knowledge that some Texans in high power planned an investigation in Texas. The belief that the President's death might have been the result of Communist influence or plot was at first sufficient to begin planning a Grand Jury investigation. Such plans alarmed Hoover enough, and subsequently his personal friend, the new President Lyndon Baines Johnson, for either or both of the men to deliver a demand of no official state investigation. That demand led to the speedy formation of the Warren Commission in December, 1963. The Commission held its first meetings in January of 1964.

The liberty of the Fourth Estate was established, according to the United States Constitution, to protect the people from abuses of the government. The failure of Dallas' major newspapers to fulfill their mission, was, if not the greatest misdeed, certainly a significant omission blocking further investigation.

In this book, I shall invoke the license of writing "docufiction" (fiction which has a base in reality) to suggest realities which might have become public knowledge. The author defends the use of this medium. It is dissimilar to "evidence", which is accepted as fact by a multitude of readers. Such "evidence" is often a mixture of conjecture and partially verifiable fact. Docufiction does not confuse conjecture with verifiable fact. It leaves the reader free to weigh the plausibility of the various scenarios.

And to those who would say they never allow themselves to speculate or be influenced by suggestion, I ask: Have you never watched television "news"? Have you never seen the alternate stories of "Amy Fisher"?

The method employed by the author will be criticized. The episodes within did not actually happen. The dialogues which follow transpire in a reporter's setting where the aforementioned constitutional ideal is met. Where duty was to probe the ground for signs of pure water or contaminated waste.

To this end, I employ techniques similar to those I used when writing a series alone. In the past, I probed into several problem areas, often posing as a friend to those I suspected. At times I established a pattern of guilt by checking subjects at random times without revealing my intent. I would ask one or two trusted friends, usually people who were not employed as reporters, to cooperate. One would investigate those I suspected to be guilty and the other scrutinized those I believed were not involved. Another method which worked for me, when in an unfamiliar area was to interrogate persons in the field, e.g. racial discrimination, who were not at the top. Rather, they merely worked near the activity under investigation. Amazing how often loose talk reaches the ears of innocents, because they are not believed to be a threat.

In what follows, I create an investigative team consisting of three reporters, two male and one female. We shall call them Jim, Ben and Beth. Jim will hold the title of general assignments reporter with the backup police beat (identical to that held by Jim Koethe). Ben will be regional reporter (a beat commonly held by one reporter who assured readership of the full circulation region of a metropolitan newspaper). At the *Dallas Times Herald*, a region would have included Big Springs, Greenville, Allen, Irving and even south to Duncanville. While the small cities had their own newspapers, weeklies or dailies, the metropolitan daily was also read. The third reporter, Beth, is the medical reporter, a critical "beat" for a member of this team. The team members would first decide which events and persons aligned with their beats, or personal knowledge.

For Jim the following assignments would have been logical:

- Police bungling
- Eye witness knowledge
- Knowledge of Lee Harvey Oswald by authorities
- The killing of Officer J.D. Tippit

Ben would been essential in covering the following areas:

- Infiltrating the right wing in the greater Dallas area
- Networking among law enforcement officials throughout the Dallas area
- Uncovering contributors to the investigation who were stationed on the periphery, and would only have talked if given the shield of anonymity

Beth would have been valuable in the following areas:

- Locating personnel at Parkland Hospital who would describe the President's injuries and events related to his futile treatment
- Talking to family members and personal friends of Lee Oswald, including the emigres
- Obtaining views on Oswald's psychiatric state from her contacts in the psychiatric community

The investigative team members would have known they stood in a precarious position with their employers, the publishers, and would surely have encountered envy and derision among their peers. Assume that this team accomplished its mission, in whole or in part, and kept the citizenry informed and protected from deceit.

"Dateline Dallas" is written in vignette form. It is not fully formed fiction as in a novel.

Eleven

Dateline Dallas, November 29

The newspaper lunch room was sterile and uninteresting, pepped up only by the orange-red molded plastic booth seats. Vending machines covered a full wall, some serving coffee or soda pop. An automat with revolving trays offered dry sandwiches, oranges and hard boiled eggs. It could have been the *Dallas Times Herald*.

A few minutes after 6 p.m., when most reporters have left for the day, Ben drank black coffee while Beth sipped a Coke. They waited for Jim to return from the police station. Beth looked at Ben's face, wondering how he usually seemed cheerful, even when silent.

"I wonder how Oswald did it, if he did," Beth mused.

Ben glanced sharply at her. "Do you know anything about guns?"

Her gaze rested on the Coke bottle. Slowly she rubbed her fingers downward over the condensation from the cold drink, forming a wet ring at the bottle's base. "Nope," she admitted. "But it sounds strange to me for a man to go to work, and actually do his job, apparently competently, and still plan to polish off the President during the lunch hour." She shook her head.

Ben laughed. "Well, that's one way to look at it. You'll be the one looking at mental competency. But there's another way."

Beth gazed into Ben's brown eyes and fair skinned face. His curly, rust colored hair made him the darling of women in and outside the newspaper. He obviously enjoyed it.

Leaning forward on his elbows Ben looked seriously at Beth. "My dad collects guns, rifles especially. There's a lot of hunting around Big Springs. He told me over the weekend that he saw a rifle similar to Oswald's at a flea market."

"Did he buy it?" she asked.

"Hell no," Ben said. "The damn bolt action hung up half the time. He said it wasn't reliable enough."

They paused as Jim, his coat tail flapping as he rounded the corner, took long, quick strides toward them. He slid his long limbs into the booth beside Ben.

The two reporters gave Jim their attention. He had first mentioned the series to the city editor and fiercely argued with other editors until they grudgingly gave him permission to assemble a team. They had been given permission only to work on the series for four weeks, and had to cover their assigned beats as well. Jim became team leader and chose Beth and Ben to work with him. Both were enthusiastic and secretly flattered, ignoring the unavoidable extra work.

Now both reporters turned to Jim. He frowned and looked at each of them scornfully. "Did I just hear you say 'Oswald's rifle'?"

Ben's face turned sour. "Maybe. You got x-ray ears?"

Jim slid down and leaned his head back against the seat. "All I mean is that if we start out accepting everything that's been said, we're sunk already. I'm not saying it is, or that it isn't."

"I stand corrected," Ben said with mock humility. "But we ought to talk about what we should accept first."

Beth stepped into the breach between the others. "I agree. Jim was closest to the scene. I was here doing rewrite. Ben was at Parkland. Where I should have been," she added.

"Only because I was closer," Ben said in his defense. "I was still at Love Field waiting for the President to get back. The desk had me interviewing everyone from the control tower people down to baggage handlers. How do you handle a Presidential touchdown?" His voice grew deep, sounding authoritative. Then it became high pitched as he mimicked his interviewees. "We just got everybody out of the way, and they told us what to do." Ben added with a shrug, "I was an afterthought. Of course, I did get everybody's residence. Kind of amazing how many people from Big Springs and other burbs commute to Dallas every day."

Even Jim, now sympathetic, down-played his role. "And I miss the actual shots while I'm chasing Bob Jackson's film across the street."

Beth joined in their soft chuckles, but cut it short. "I need to know how you feel about my story with the doctors. I feel 99% positive Perry was comfortable that the neck wound was an entrance wound."

Jim rubbed his eyes, a shock of dark blonde hair falling across his forehead. Pushing his hair back, he looked at her. "We're only going to be able to investigate for three weeks. The fourth, we write. So, unless we find other evidence that contradicts what he said to you, I say we accept it."

"Good," she said, "because he's starting to have second thoughts. People in Washington are leaning on several of the emergency room doctors."

"That's my point," Jim said. "We have to write a Dallas story. We haven't got time for more. I had a hard enough time selling the brass that we should even write the series. I don't believe," he said in a sarcastic tone, "they'll okay an expense voucher for the Soviet Union."

Ben pointed an aggressive finger at them both. "Or even New Orleans. That's where Oswald was born and went to a lot."

"Right," Jim agreed. "Here's what I suggest. It's been a week since the assassination. I want to nose around my contacts at the police station, talk to the witnesses and find out what I can about Tippit.

There's already talk that he was into some hanky panky. Beth should start on her Parkland contacts and try to get close to Oswald's family." He looked hard into her brown eyes. "I know that's a tall order."

She only shrugged, unsurprised.

Jim continued, "Ben, can your father help us out?"

Beth thought about what little she knew about Ben's family. His father was postmaster at Big Springs, and well placed politically. He also knew guns. She knew nothing more.

Ben grinned. "You want me to run home to daddy?" It was his turn to shrug. "I agree he can probably help a lot. I don't see any problems there. He'll be glad to pick up a Carcano and experiment with it."

Jim pulled a notebook from his pocket but only began to doodle on a blank page. "My problem is that Curry and Fritz ain't talking. The story is that Hoover or maybe even Lyndon told them to shut up."

Ben asked, "Could you get an interview with Henry Wade or Barefoot Sanders? I hear Sanders is saying there may be a Texas investigation."

"Maybe Wade." Jim sat straight in the booth, fully a head taller than Ben. His customary look was that of extraordinary confidence. Not a traditionally handsome man, he was instead charismatic.

Beth felt acceptance toward both Jim and Ben. There was even a certain romantic attraction toward them. Her feelings were, however, greatly tempered by an unhappy first marriage to a reporter. She had decided that reporters did not make good husbands. She openly vowed that if she ever married again it would be to a "civilian". The kidding she received was good natured, and she wanted it to stay that way. Not that Jim or Ben had ever asked her for a date–she was too straight and narrow for their tastes. She turned her thoughts back to the story. "What about Ruby?"

Ben jumped in first. "He's so unpredictable that I can't see any inconsistency in what he did."

Jim looked at Beth and took the lead. "Beth told me the problem with that. She saw the television shot where Oswald seemed to give Ruby a look of recognition. And, of course, we know how close Oswald was to his apartment...only blocks away for God's sake."

"Several of us think Ruby was going to help him get out of town or give him a payoff," Beth said. She hastily added, "if Oswald was involved."

Jim said, "Let's pass on that 'til next week. The whole police force is under scrutiny over how Ruby got into the basement." He laughed and added, "I'd be surprised if he wasn't there."

"And when he wasn't there, the police were drinking it up at his club," Ben said.

After clearing his throat, Jim spoke slowly. "I'll ask Jim Featherston to put in a good word for me with Wade. Then I've a whole string of eyewitnesses. Some who saw two men on that floor, at least that's what they say, and I've got to interview them all. I don't want them to forget details. That happens damn quick. Next they start inventing."

"Beth, see what the nurses and orderlies say at Parkland, but I want more than one good psychiatric opinion of Oswald's actions Friday. And don't let them assume that Oswald killed Tippit. Ben, you get onto that 'el cheapo' gun. Could it have been the murder weapon, excluding others? Then we meet Tuesday, Thursdays and Saturdays, and in between if needed to pool our stuff. This week, I think we'd better get together in two days...see if we have any conflicts."

Ben and Beth nodded. Beth said, "I talked to Bob Jackson for awhile."

"We know he saw the rifle barrel in the window," Ben said.

"Yes, but he told me that it was drawn in slowly. And he believes the shots he heard came not from high, or low. He can't pin it down closer than that." Ben grunted while Jim played with his pen. Jim's glance at her was questioning. "You know him pretty well. Does he like to grandstand?"

"The opposite," Beth said firmly. "What Jackson says he saw and heard, is exactly that. He'll never make up a story. It has to be there."

Jim took charge again, "Then let's quit wasting time." He swung his legs from the booth and loped ahead of then into the newsroom and toward the elevators.

Ben looked at Beth with a twinkle in his eyes. They slid out of the booth and took their time walking toward the elevators. Ben mockingly sung the theme to the Lone Ranger. Beth shook her head. "I hope Jim never makes city editor."

Ben shook his head. "That'll never happen. The brass don't like him a whit. He's just too good to fire." Once out the back door, he gave her a quick salute. Lights outlined the few remaining cars in the dark open parking lot.

Beth waved back with confidence. What a chance they had!

Twelve

Wednesday Gloom

The booth had become their own. The lunch room was deserted this night. One sandwich a day, void of mustard or mayonnaise, was enough even for reporters.

Jim shook his head. He had loosened his tie and rolled up his shirt sleeves. "Those damn witnesses. Every damn one that gives a good story turns around and fowls it up by sticking in something they couldn't have seen. And the police lineups, especially the first one manufactured for that Markum woman. I got a police clerk to tell me, like it was a joke, that he put on striped suspenders another guy had worn that day. And then they all give phony names and addresses and Oswald just says who he is and where he worked. Real positive identification," he said sarcastically.

"Still, it's not bad for our story," Beth said.

"I guess not," Jim admitted. "I know it's too early to make any judgment. But I have the feeling that we're going to find facts stranger than fiction throughout this investigation."

"Dad got a Carcano, and he has a kid who's a real sharp shooter startin' to make some simulations," Ben said.

"At a moving target?" Jim asked.

"No." Ben chuckled. "I don't think they can get anybody to sit in a moving car and turn their backs on a rifle."

Beth spoke slowly. "Well, Marina should be moving back in with Ruth Paine in a day or so. I may get to see her. But from what I hear, she's given every story the Secret Service or the FBI wanted, and some they hadn't even thought of."

"Naturally," Jim said. "What's Paine like?"

"Squeaky clean," Beth said instantly.

With mock horror, Ben's eyes bulged. "If you think she's squeaky clean, she must be a saint."

"Saint Paine," Jim said and laughed.

Beth squirmed slightly, but spoke up firmly. "No. I think she's maybe some kind of government agent. She and her husband are separated, but he comes over or contacts her every week. They seem to be 'working together'."

Jim asked, "Do you think you can get any evidence or proof?"

Beth saddened. "No, I really don't. That's the most careful woman I ever met. She's friendly, but doesn't miss a trick. She told me she turned some mail over to the FBI that Lee didn't pick up Thursday night. I asked her what it was, and she just tilted her nose in the air and said, 'I respected Lee's privacy. I just put it in a stack and didn't look at return addresses'."

"But I have found one emigre who'll talk. In fact, he doesn't stop talking. Name's DeMohrenschildt. Baron, in fact," Beth said without enthusiasm.

"Why the glum?" Ben asked. "Is he a phony?" He knew Beth well enough to know when she didn't trust her source.

"Yes and no. I talked to him over the phone and he took up 45 minutes just telling me that he would discuss himself and Oswald. I think I'll go around the world with him and still not know the most vital information. But I've got an appointment tomorrow night." She turned to Jim, who was being unusually quiet. "What have you found out about Tippit?"

Jim seemed uncharacteristically reticent. "Only that he's been having an affair–and that isn't what I'm looking for. I have to start over on that one, and damn it, I don't have the time. There's another angle. Oswald may not have had time to reach Tippit to be his killer." He cupped his chin in one hand, his expression seemingly depressed.

Ben instantly offered his services to help Jim look into the time element of the Tippit shooting. After thinking for a moment, the star of the group, always the lone wolf, accepted Ben's offer. They had begun to think and act as a team.

Looking at Ben, Jim said, "Okay, and there's something else. Roy Truly may know something he's not telling. Do you think you could get in the back door at the book building?"

Ben grinned. "Is this going to cost me a bundle and make me listen to rock'n roll all night at some dive ?"

"Probably," Jim admitted with a sly grin.

They parted company for the week, each less alone than when he or she began the meeting.

Thirteen

Week Three

Dateline Dallas, December 9, 1963

Moods somber, Jim, Beth and Ben chewed sandwiches and drank pop at their table. It was late in the evening, and none had found time to get a full meal on most days since they had last met.

Grimacing as he downed the bitter coffee, Jim said, "We need to meet somewhere else. I'm tired of the stares we're getting." He glared at a young reporter seated several tables away, but possibly in hearing distance. The reporter grinned back at him, obviously interested in the scene he was privy to. Ben said, "We can meet at my apartment, if you clean up after yourselves."

Jim laughed aloud. "What makes you so proud of a garage apartment with a drippy faucet?"

"Actually, I like my claw footed bathtub, the birds outside the windows, and even my old landlady. She sometimes gives me leftovers," Ben said. "Anyway, take it or leave it. Old Highland Park's close and it's quiet."

Jim grunted affirmatively, and Beth breathed a brief sigh that no controversy had arisen. In their brief meetings over the past four days, Jim had been testy and even sarcastic. Ben would begin calmly enough, but turn quickly abrasive in Jim's presence. She knew they all felt pushed to the hilt. It was like chipping away at brick walls with their fingernails.

Jim had to gripe once more. "Quint's making me do even more straight police coverage since," and he mimicked. "Since I'm out somewhere all the time anyway."

Ben said mildly, "What bothers me even more is that the desk is still giving stories to other people. Lehrer and Schmidt were checking out a call from a gun shop owner. Why don't they give them to us? Besides, I had to cover the new design for a water district at Duncanville, and that took an entire day."

Beth grinned at Ben. "Was it exciting?"

Ben leered at her. "I almost had an orgasm when the lady mayor talked about 'all that good, clean water'."

Jim began to derisively compare the merits of his work with Ben's. Beth listened until she couldn't stand it any longer. She barked, "Shut up, you two. Where the hell are we now? Granted, we all have too much to do. But those unsolicited calls aren't proving valid. Let them cover the crap. That's not the point."

Her voice softened as she said, "I may have a nurse who will talk. The doctors have lost their voices. I hear the Washington autopsy doctors contacted those at Parkland. None of them will talk. I'll make you a bet that the Dallas doctors change stories. And I know who'll be the first. Except maybe one resident I ran into today. He wasn't in ER but he's heard plenty in the doctor's lounge. And I talked to a psychiatrist and a psychologist in private practice and we'll get our psychological report."

"Get the nurse's interview as soon as you can," Jim said in a normal tone. "I hope we get someone who will let us use their name. That's my trouble right now."

Beth nodded. "More about Ruth Paine. She's pretty much the link with the press for Marina. I saw Marina and we got a photo. Ruth interpreted while Marina told everybody how sorry she is. I got a story from Ruth Paine. She's pretty accessible. The thing is... Marina didn't live with her as long as we've heard. She lived with other emigres some of the time."

"I helped some of them get medical care in the past and I think they'll give me stories. George DeMohrenschildt is strange, and so is his wife. They went through Central America with their cameras hidden under a cloth on top of a mule."

Jim asked, "What do they say they were doing?"

Beth's mouth twisted. "Collecting rocks. Really. He's a geologist. But, of course the rocks were almost all lost when they stumbled onto American soldiers and heard about the Bay of Pigs." Her voice became deeply mysterious. "They barely escaped with their lives."

"How interesting," Ben said. "And they have no contact with the American government?"

Beth said, "I told you I thought it was going to be like that. But I'm still talking to them." She changed the subject. "But before I talk to them again, I'm going to protect you pathetic, overworked guys and interview Marguerite Oswald. She's beginning to beg for publicity."

"Isn't she a nut?" Ben asked.

"Maybe, maybe not. But she's Oswald's mother. And isn't he the only suspect we've got?"

Jim mumbled, "Yeah. But from the eye witnesses' stories, and even Decker's, I'm thinking the frontal shots came from back of the picket fence. If Oswald's a patsy," he said, emphasizing the "if", "and shots came from the fence area, those shooters aren't hanging around Dallas. Police officers stationed on the overpass admit there was considerable traffic in the railroad yards. And the fence was unprotected, at least by local cops. A couple of witnesses ran up there and got stopped by a guy who says he was Secret Service. Sorrels said he didn't have anybody back there...at least not under his supervision."

Ben said, "At least we've got near-proof that Oswald couldn't have made it to Tippit in time to kill him."

"At least not without reasonable doubt," Jim murmured in agreement.

"I think our approach could turn out to be," Jim said, emphasizing the word "could", "that Oswald at least was not the lone assassin."

"I'd settle for that," Ben said.

"Maybe you would, but I won't...I want more," Jim said emphatically.

Ben only shrugged, then said, "The kid that's working with Dad has tested three Carcanos everyday. Even under great conditions, he can't match two or three shots that quickly with any accuracy. And Dad still says he's the best."

"But I may have some stuff that's even hotter. Let me follow it up and let's meet Saturday at my place."

Beth leaned toward him. "Hot as fire? Maybe we'd better talk about it now."

Ben's face developed a closed expression...unlike him. "Not yet," he said.

Jim raised his eyebrow at Beth. "My goodness, he's even got me interested."

She put her notebook in her purse and closed the clasp. "My point is that we can't afford to get in dangerous situations. We could lose the whole story."

Ben turned mockingly cheerful and sneered. "Or our lives. Put on my tombstone: 'He died for a cause. No one knows what, because they killed him first'."

Jim regarded Ben silently. Beth snapped, "That's not funny." For once, she was the first to leave the group.

Fourteen

Week Three, Day Seven

Dateline Dallas, December 14, 1963

Shadows spotted the walls of Ben's one-room apartment atop a frame garage in old Highland Park. Leaves still clinging to the live oak and maples trees on the large lot were in the last stages of withered green. Some were brown but still hung by shriveled twigs to tree branches, awaiting the first icy blast of cold weather, signifying winter in Dallas.

The garage and apartment sat well to the rear on the acre holding an old brick two story home, once a mansion for the Hartford family. Now it was occupied by Geneva Hartford, the last direct descendant of a wealthy oil baron, Hugh Hartford. The big house still had servants, but live-in help was scarce now. Ben was a reporter. But not unlike other young men who had lived there–many students at Southern Methodist University–he knew that in exchange for the modest rent, he was a passive body guard for the estate and its lone aged occupant.

A large window air conditioner cooled the area adequately but made a racket. Jim complained briefly until Beth shot him a silencing glance. She wasn't going to let the bickering begin today.

They sat in wooden chairs around a green painted wooden kitchen table with a white porcelain top. There was a free standing sink, another wooden utility table, intended for food preparation, and a roll top wooden kitchen cabinet which stored the few pots, plates and glasses

Ben had cared to acquire. Like Ben, Beth admired its antique charm. Any romance about the apartment was lost on Jim who lived in an apartment similar to all others lining Gaston Avenue leading from east Dallas to downtown. In that area, occupants moved so often it had been dubbed "suitcase city".

They passed around two psychiatric reports Beth had acquired from a psychologist and a psychiatrist. Both, although often using different terminology, described Lee Harvey Oswald as either Schizoid or a personality disorder. Both noted that a definitive examination would have required the presence of Lee Harvey Oswald. Jim complained, "Don't they know we'd like to have him here, too?" Beth hushed him with the explanation that the professionals had used standard psychiatric procedures for writing the reports.

"These are damn good reports," Ben noted.

Beth agreed. "The best we could possibly get with his erratic history. Furthermore, I agree with them."

Ben pulled several pages of papers out of a manila envelope. "Now this is really top secret. If we use any of it, we have to protect the source by going to jail if we have to."

Jim commented, "They're not sending reporters to jail as much lately. But we know who it is. I'm prepared to protect the source."

"Yes, him," Ben said firmly, "but also others in the postal service".

Jim asked, "Is this what you were referring to the other day?"

Ben nodded, and lay two pages on the table top as Jim and Beth leaned forward. "Copies of orders for a Carcano from Alek Hidell", Ben said. "And they're postmarked." He then stacked several other papers beside them. "And here are changes of address–Dallas and new Orleans. I didn't get to travel to New Orleans but this stuff came from both cities. And here's the clincher–as least for me. This note," he said pulling the last photocopy from the envelope. He laid it squarely in the middle of the table. Beth squirmed closer to Jim's side so they both could view the dim document copy together. "A passport application."

Jim asked, "How the hell did you get this?" His voice showed admiration.

Ben shrugged. "Look at the directions, right hand side. Beth read: 'Mail passport to Mr. Lee H. Oswald, 3124 west 5th St., Fort Worth, Texas'. But this wasn't mailed there..." she said. looking puzzled.

"No," Ben said. "But the passport was. You guys don't know how much postal inspectors see. Just for fun, Jim, you ought to watch the magazines you order. 'Thrills for Adventurous Men', and 'Adventures in Bedrooms and Other Sequestered Places'." Ben adopted a pompous air, then grinned. "Just tried it on you to check out the system."

Jim looked faintly uncomfortable. "They come in brown wrappers," he said defensively.

Beth said, "Move on–let's look at the other side." The passport application asked for the purpose of the trip. Both Beth and Jim squinted at the words squeezed together in the box. He read: "To attend the College of A. Schwetzier Switzerland and the University of Turkey. To all other countries as a tourist. Guess he meant Schweitzer." Then he read a list of eight from Cuba to Russia and France.

Next, Ben placed a brief statement atop the document stating that Oswald was scheduled to be released from Active Duty on 11 September, 1959. Beth glanced back at the passport "The application's dated September 4, 1959. God this man had some connections."

"He got a hardship discharge," Ben said.

"That's what Marguerite said, too." Beth agreed.

"I have a contribution, too," Jim said. He reached in his inside coat pocket for an envelope.

"I feel like I just failed show and tell," Beth said.

It was Ben and Beth's turn to lean over the copy of a small note. It was addressed to Mr. Hunt. "I am not ready to proceed until I have further directions." Lee H. Oswald"

Beth asked, "H.L. Hunt?"

Jim said, "Dunno. He says not, according to my source. But he was interested enough to keep a copy. This is a copy of what Hunt kept. It definitely raises questions." His glance turned toward Ben. "And it didn't arrive by mail," he said.

Ben nodded. "Neither did all this. Dad has good Army connections, too."

"I don't think," Jim said, "I'd be too comfortable being your father right now."

Ben nodded in agreement. "But he's more worried about you two than anything else. He's used to this stuff, and I grew up knowing what I could talk about and what I couldn't. It just firmed up my ambition."

Beth asked, "What is it?"

"To own a small town newspaper. I'll tell everything I know, or anybody tells me. I'm tired of secrets." His youthful face was tired, but determined.

Jim looked at the hand writing on the passport application. "It seems to match what I've seen at the police station. I finally got a really green rookie cop who works under Lt. Day to admit he doesn't think they found any definite fingerprints on the rifle. Just old smudges. He's getting me copies of anything like evidence they've got. Claims he didn't see any clip with the rifle. They've got photo copies of two Selective Service cards—one for Oswald and one for Hidell. I don't think the handwriting on the Hidell card is Oswald's but I could be wrong. The cops say Washington says it is."

"Say, did everybody get a chance to hear that story from the radio station in New Orleans? They really seem hungry for publicity. Apparently he played two sides of the political fence there."

"Here, too," Beth said. "He talked Marxism but his acquaintances were right wing. Ruth Paine's husband is moderate, maybe, but his father's leftist. And he admitted he took Oswald to a Civil Liberties

Union meeting. And get this. Michael Paine designs helicopters but he only has a high school education." She chuckled. "I'm glad I'm not riding in them."

She quickly sobered. "He did have some impressive college but never graduated." She switched topics. "Most of the emigres are right wing, but they don't have much to do with General Walker and the Birch group. And from what I hear from them, DeMohrenschildt is on everybody's side. He was the only one of that group that had much to do with Lee Oswald. Marina was the darling of that group–especially the men."

Jim pushed his chair back and put hands behind his head, again taking charge. "Oswald was, and I really believe this, establishing what they call a 'legend'. He can't be pinned down to anything."

Ben echoed the thought. "He may have shot at Walker, but there's no way to know why. And by the way, I found the secretary you told I was the hottest thing since a hot potato. I definitely paid my dues. So you owe me one. She wanted to go to the Cellar. I couldn't hear for two days."

Jim grew interested. "Did she have anything to say?"

"She said the FBI called Truly before he placed the ad. She listened in on the switchboard. According to her, they asked Truly to place an ad for order clerks. He argued that he didn't really need any...the agent said it would only be temporary."

Jim's voice came out in staccato bursts. "That's what I thought. But let's leave the Walker thing alone...even the DPD didn't buy his story. They think Walker just wanted publicity. And a neighbor saw two cars around Walker's place. But Truly's gal has given us good information."

Beth asked "How did he know to apply? And does that make him the assassin?"

Jim's voice returned to normal. "You can be sure he found out in the most innocent way. And he did need a job real bad. He may not even have known that he was supposed to apply. And it certainly doesn't make him the assassin. But it suggests that the feds wanted him at that cruddy book building."

Ben asked, "Did Truly finger Oswald?"

"Yeah," Jim said, "but it wasn't the first APB. It was after Fritz got there."

"The first APB was a bad description," Ben said.

Beth interrupted, "Gimme a cookie," she demanded. Ben passed a sack over. "Gimme, gimme," he said and grinned. The three reporters had passed bickering and could almost read each other's thoughts. Ben, too, fished out a chocolate chip cookie and sipped some milk. Jim was, as usual, drinking coffee.

Ben looked at both of them. "Are you aware how many police officers are in the army reserve, and how many of them are Birchers and even KKK members?"

Jim nodded silently. Beth murmured that she hadn't been aware of it. "That's why," Jim said, "I don't trust a lot of the police evidence. They had plenty of opportunity to plant it at Oswald's rooming house or even at the Paine's. And you can be sure Michael Paine didn't give a whit. And we have LIFE Magazine getting everything valuable, especially that movie film. Check out their influence. It's gigantic, and it's right wing."

Ben looked silently at his papers for a few seconds before he said, "I can check out some of the Minutemen and see what they're saying."

Jim said, "Do it ver-r-r-y carefully. They're lethal."

Ben nodded and said, "I know. I'll proceed with caution."

"I can't get Marina to say a thing now," Beth commented.

"She's already said exactly what the feds wanted her to say," Jim said firmly. "Think of it. She's under guard...excuse me, protection."

The tone was sarcastic. "And don't think for a minute she's not afraid of deportation. She knows she's safer here. She remembers Soviet methods."

"So," Ben said, his voice low, "Do we agree? Oswald was a government agent. U.S. government I mean?"

Jim nodded solemnly. "He worked for whoever needed him. And for sure, he never knew the whole story. He was low level, and expendable."

Beth sighed. "Just what his mother says. Except for the last part–and I wish she didn't ever have to hear it."

"But she will," Jim said blandly. He pushed back his shoulders and stretched his arms. They were reaching a point where he could feel the tension inside. He wanted to reach out and grab answers that weren't available yet. For a minute he allowed himself to speculate. "I feel sure that Oswald didn't do it. He may have set the stage. In a trial he would have walked, even through it was the President who got killed. No doubt in my mind. But since Ruby carried out orders and silenced Oswald for good, we've got to find real good stuff that proves there were other people who could have done it. And done it better. That's the best we can do for the poor slob."

"Don't call him that," Beth said. She ducked her head. "I wish we could clear him."

"Not enough time," Jim said. "Listen, do we have any contacts inside the telephone company?"

Ben, too, stretched and said, "Now don't laugh. My mother. She runs the phone company at Big Springs."

Jim smiled. Beth's voice held wonder, "Your family is a veritable gold mine of information. I don't know how..."

Ben interrupted. "Look, they've got the jobs they have because of politics. But they're still good people."

"Never doubted it," Jim said. "And what we need now will never be traced to her."

"What might that be?" Ben asked with resignation.

"The phone records of Jack Ruby."

"For how long?" Ben asked.

"Oh, the last two or three months."

"I'll see what I can do," Ben said.

Beth looked worried, as she nibbled at the cookie. "Aren't we in pretty deep by now?"

Jim's face stretched into the wide grin he flashed as his most charming self. "We always have been. And it ain't over yet."

Fifteen

Week Four

Dateline Dallas, December 17, 1963

Twigs from the barren trees outside Ben's window scratched at the glass of Ben's apartment windows. The weak version of winter had settled over Dallas. Some days were still hot, but others, especially when high wind blew, were bitterly cold.

The team sat around the table, now piled high with papers. The air conditioner was silent. A square gas heater in the corner sent warm air mostly toward the ceiling, but the reporters were oblivious to their surroundings.

Beth held center. "He's just a resident, but he says he'll give us his story. He says the clan of physicians will deny it. But I say we should take it. He'll probably have to leave Dallas, at least I warned him of that possibility, but from what I see, he has several other choices."

"He says most of those in ER said they were frontal shots...and he won't change his mind. He's a brassy young guy but I can stand that, 'cause I think he'll stick to his story."

Jim cut her short. "We have to use some of the witnesses' testimony, weak as it is. I think Carolyn Walthers is the best bet, even over Rowland. That establishes two men in the windows. I don't even think it calls the others a liar. They say they saw a man, but that doesn't mean they saw everything."

"That part's really coming together. My interview with the motorcycle cop will make people sit up and think. But I think they're wrong about Tippit and Oswald being in it together. It'll cast doubt that Oswald would have killed him. And we want all the doubt we can get."

Ben pulled three sheets of paper from his pocket. "Here are the phone numbers you wanted." He handed the papers to Jim, who glanced down the list and said, "My, my, how many calls to Chicago! Checking this out will send my phone bill through the roof. But I think Campisi's cooked Ruby's goose as the 'lone patriot'."

Ben added, "Isn't Ruby making sounds like this might not have been his idea?"

Jim nodded but added, "Right now his lawyers are silencing him, but I think he'll open up after our series. How is it going with the Minutemen?"

Beth could feel the tension in the room. Ben's face was impassive. "I've got a gut feeling that I've stumbled onto something really big. But there is absolutely no way to prove it." He sighed in frustration.

"Do you think they did the shooting?"', Jim asked.

"Well first look at it this way," Ben said. "They're extremely well trained. They'll take orders from military men who are coincidentally radically right wing. I can't do a survey, but the police, who played a part, at least after the shooting, are also radically right. Even those Captains and Lieutenants. But they aren't experts with rifles for the most part. Generally, they deal in hand guns. Now, back to the Minutemen. There is a group here. They are trained. They are capable of scoring shots in adverse conditions. And they'll do anything the military, or even the reserve, tells them to do...on orders."

Jim interrupted. "What have you got any of them to say, if anything?"

Ben looked down at his clenched hands in his lap. "Oh, I got an interview, one with a name and everything. The greenest, youngest one I could find. He's a sitting duck. Said the crack team just finished up 'an assignment'. That's the reason he was so casual when he talked to me. He told me how proud he was when Colonel West and some General from Oklahoma reviewed them. They passed with flying colors. They were told they were America's best defense against foreign military forces."

Jim frowned. "Printing that shouldn't hang him, I wouldn't think."

Ben threw his head back and stared at his ceiling as if he had never seen it before. "Not if I don't add what he told me at the last. The kid just blurted out, 'Course I didn't go with them when they went to special training. I'm too new'."

"Where did they go?"

"He didn't know. The brass just up and left camp with the crack team—six of them. They left, with their gear, but not their uniforms, on November 18 and returned on November 25. Without the brass. And I got records that prove members of the team were not in camp."

Silence fell over them, as each dealt with Ben's information.

Jim cracked, "We may all be dead meat."

Beth asked, "Are we doing the right thing, to include his story?"

Both men were slow to answer. Jim spoke in as caring a tone as he could muster. "Look we're reporters. He didn't have to tell the story. And we aren't the jury who'll decide whether it's true."

Ben nodded slowly. "I have to admit that I agree."

Standing up and reaching for his coat, Jim signaled that the meeting had ended. They lingered a few minutes more, as though they were reluctant to part.

Jim said, "I've got telephone calls to check. Let's meet Thursday and bring everything you've got—even background research. I'll bring everything that I have to date on the Great Southwest Corporation. It looks like Marina may not have to be controlled by the feds. Ole Big D may handle everything for her."

Ben remarked, "I looked up some of that on another assignment several months ago, and I couldn't find much. Where's your contact?"

Jim shrugged. "I'd like to say it's local authority, but I can't. I was having the same trouble you did, and what with everything else I'm trying to dig up, I called an old college friend. She works in the morgue at the Washington Star. They've got a lot more stuff than we have. After all, some of the investigations are local news for them. They're reliable, too."

"But let's see what we have, then take sections and start to write. I want it turned in by the 19th. Quint says the Warren Commission's getting local depositions, and they got subpoena power. We want to hit the streets before they do."

Ben chuckled and said, "You mean I'm going to get my kitchen table back?"

Joining in the banter, Jim said, "I'll even buy you a new one. Wood'n everything."

Ben grinned. "Forget it. Just leave it like you found it."

As they buttoned their coats and lightly joked, Beth thought to herself: *It may mean a lot, or they'll say we're off our rockers.* She had a half wish that they hadn't found as much as they had... no. They had to do it.

Sixteen

End of Week Four

Dateline Dallas, December 19, 1963

Three heads bent low over the plethora of papers which covered the top of the porcelain table. The voices were low. Occasionally one would pull a paper from a stack where it had been piled in error. After five hours of work, with only a brief break for sandwiches, they agreed they were making progress.

Beth stood up first.."I need to stretch." Ben gratefully rose and fell onto his sofa on his stomach. Jim stretched out on the blanket covering Ben's bed, spread-eagled. Beth paced the floor and glanced at Jim. His arms and legs were so long he covered almost the entire bed.

"I see these papers in my sleep," she remarked.

"I know," Jim said. "Let's see what we can prioritize without looking at them."

Ben turned his head toward Jim's direction. "That's a scientific way to look at it," he said with sarcasm.

Jim just laughed. "Don't worry...we face the truth next."

Beth, probably the most organized of the three began, "We've got enough to suggest that Oswald was a government agent, low level. We also can establish that he was interested in getting guns by mail. The psychiatric report establishes him as a personality disorder, but he didn't even act like a psycho on the 22nd. He had right and left wing contacts, pro-Castro and against."

Jim broke in, "–the legend."

"Right," Beth said in agreement. "We have some missing blocks of time. The only one that bothers me was Mexico."

"Don't worry about it," Jim said. "We're not writing a book, though we've got enough for one. After we write the first of the series outlining what we're going to cover, we go right to Oswald."

Both Ben and Beth murmured agreement.

Ben said, "Then we cover the motorcade and its flaws. That let's us start on the military involvement."

Jim interrupted, "I think you're too far ahead. What happened at Parkland needs to be worked into the intro because if they had obeyed Texas law, we'd have an autopsy that might make sense. We need to include the stray bullet on the gurney. I'll bet a dollar to a doughnut that it's a plant. Maybe by Ruby. I believe Seth Kantor's story completely. We just give bare bones on the military in the intro. Then Beth's interview with the nurse and resident come next, what happened at Parkland. Then the military."

"Okay," Ben nodded in agreement.

"Then back to Dallas, it's politics, Big D style. Great Southwest influence. Marina's got a lawyer and guess who he's with? Great Southwest. And who represents Great Southwest? Bedford Wynne. And who's he connected with? The Murchisons. And where did Marina end up staying? At the Inn of the Six Flags. Owned by Great Southwest. And who's in trouble right now, or at least he was this summer? Wynne. He had an army audit of his salary from Sweetwater Development. Who set up Sweetwater Development? Murchison's Tecon Company, by and through the firm of Wynne, Jaffe, and Tinsley. Incidentally, Wynne's mixed up with Bobby Baker, and he always means trouble."

Beth grinned and shook her head. "Call me dumb. I wondered, but didn't want to ask, why at the very first Marina and company decided to make this a vacation and go to the Inn of Six Flags..maybe to take June on the water ride at Six Flags Over Texas? How the hell did you trace all this, Jim? That same gal at the Washington Star?"

Jim nodded and sat up. "Yeah, my friend at the Star helped. Especially on the Wynne investigation. But I got some locally, by cultivating a little higher class of Dallasite than I usually hang out with. But now let's go back to the papers and see how they pan out. Just like we said, we've got five or six, and that's a series. The fight will be getting it published...and getting the space we need."

No one spoke as they returned to the table. Only low murmurs accompanied the separation of material they couldn't substantiate or simply didn't have space for. They were working as a team. There was virtually no competition or jockeying for position. They agreed on the byline–by Jim Walls, Beth Summers and Ben Burnett–and wrote which parts of the series they would write. Jim assigned each to write the intro, and its all important lede, which they would go over when they brought their first drafts to a meeting Wednesday. That gave them ample time for revisions before the final draft, which had to be ready by December 20.

"I want all week to fight with everybody from Holcomb to Burlington," he said firmly. "And then they have to fight it out with major stockholders. That's where the action'll be." He winked at Beth before he reached for his jacket. She gave no response.

Seventeen

Page Proof

Beth, Ben and Jim leaned over the page proof after it has been read by the editors. It was all there. Jim quickly noticed that rewrite hadn't touched it. The paper was going to let them hang with this one. He began reading the story beneath the banner covering eight column of type, The banner and an overline read:

Dallas Team Cracks Cover-up
Possible JFK Assassination Conspiracy Evidence Uncovered

The story began:

By Jim Walls, Beth Summers and Ben Burnett
Staff Writers

Early reports that Lee Harvey Oswald, a deranged man, killed President John F. Kennedy from a sixth floor window of the Texas School Book Depository may be the result of a massive cover-up extending from Dallas to the nation's Capitol.

Breaking the code of secrecy which blocked any in-depth investigation into the assassination, which occurred on November 22 in Dallas' Dealey Plaza, reveals massive intrigue. Those involved possibly include Dallas civic leaders, Dallas police, the military, and segments of the American government.

In this series of five articles, the role of truthful Dallas eyewitnesses as well as some who had hidden agendas to convict one man of the heinous crime without a trial, will be detailed. As a Parkland Hospital physician said: "There wasn't any question among the doctors...they said at least one shot came from the front. And the President's face was pristine. The brain was blown away from the hairline back to the cerebellum."

Beth raised her head, turning away from the team members as they read every word of the story, which continued from the prominent front page display to page three, consuming almost half of that page. "I wonder what'll happen to us?"

Jim turned to her and grinned. "One thing I bet–Lehrer and Jackson won't be the only ones going to Washington."

"That isn't what I meant. What will happen to us after that?"

Jim wisecracked, "We better start looking for new jobs. They'll never submit us for a Pulitzer."

As we leave the fictitious team, I shall speculate over what eventually did happen to them. Jim was bought off, almost innocently, by receiving a job with a national feature magazine.

Ben Burnett was fatally injured when his car was run off a country road outside Grand Prairie, Texas. The vehicle which rammed the side of his car was never located.

Beth Summers was assigned to the Washington Bureau with the specific assignment of covering the Special Congressional Committee to Reorganize the Executive Branch of the United States Government.

PART IV

DALLAS–BIGGEST AND BEST

The mischief springs form the power which the moneyed interest derives from a paper currency which they are able to control, from the multitude of corporations with exclusive privileges which they have succeeded in obtaining...and unless you become more watchful in your States and check this spirit of monopoly and thirst for exclusive privileges you will in the end find that the most important powers of Government have been given or bartered away, and the control of your dearest interests have been passed into the hands of these corporations.

Andrew Jackson
7th President of the United States
(1768-1845)

**Dallas Times Herald reporter Connie Watson and singer Vic
Damone at a press party a the Cabana Hotel. Jack Ruby
dined at the Cabana the night of November 21, 1963.
--Publicity photo.**

Dallas Times Herald Reporters Ben Stevens, top left, and Connie Watson, top right, were first place winners in the Texas Headliners' Awards, 1965.

Jim Koethe, also a Herald reporter, died in 1964. His unsolved killing has sometimes been attributed to his JFK assassination investigation.

In Memorium...

Eighteen

Big D in the Age of Camelot

I first became a citizen of "Big D" in 1950 when I was 19 years old. I had moved there with my family from Missouri. Two years later I left to follow my new husband to Indiana, but we moved back "south" in 1954. My three children were born Dallasites. In total, I resided there 15 years, and have close family members still living in Dallas. There have been other cities and states where I domiciled–making me a fairly knowledgeable student of the varying cultures of these United States.

When we first arrived in flat, arid Dallas, my mother was called a "damn Yankee" by a neighbor, and invited to return to where she came from. I viewed the culture with a certain abstractness, never seeking the ethereal "roots", and always enjoying change.

In the 50's I was a competent legal secretary, and worked for some oilmen, the rich and those "gettin' there". Suddenly, I was emersed in a city of deeply divided economic classes and racial bias, probably a step away from the deep South where it was said 'we take good care of our Niggers'.

Our family lived in a small east Dallas section sandwiched between older homes belonging to oil men and families of established wealth, a shopping area, and a section of carefully kept middle class homes. Those sections encircled the largest man-made lake in the city, White Rock Lake. We picnicked around the lake, while a few black families dared to fish nearby. We liked to gaze at the lavish homes along Lawther Drive. All houses overlooking the lake were overshadowed by a pristine white columned home, called a "replica" of Mount Vernon. The home of famous oilman H. L. Hunt.

While we drove through many sections of Dallas there were two I seldom saw. One was west Dallas, where Blacks and some whites lived in squalor, and Oak Cliff, which was considered "lower class". We went there only to visit the city zoo. Without even realizing it, we were obeying the rules of Dallas' class structure.

Our frame home was tiny but respectable. Like any other newcomer, I soon saw and heard stories of H.L. Hunt, and even considered applying for an opening on his secretarial staff. But the Texas Employment Commission clerk warned me that he was known to "make passes" at his secretaries. I have no idea if that was fact or rumor, but believe the deciding factor in my decision not to apply rested on his well publicized right wing political stance.

I remember a family which lived "across the street" in a two bedroom frame house almost identical to the one we occupied. The woman of the house was an excellent cook, and had been raised in a home of an oil family, where her mother was a servant. She learned as a child to cook the rich, calorie laden fare that they were accustomed to. After marriage, she became a caterer.

In her frame garage were three or more electric roaster ovens, where she could and did cook several turkeys to perfection at one time. Whipped cream topped deserts and every side dish imaginable were prepared almost every day of the week, loaded into the family station wagon, and driven away to the homes of women who entertained on a regular basis.

Our neighbor, who had escaped servitude, was an established caterer, and manifestly loyal to the families she served. She never once carried stories from their homes. She had no store, did no advertising. The families knew her telephone number.

When there was just too much food to be consumed, she brought it home. If not eaten by her family in one day, she would share with us. That Mrs. "T." had brought it over was enough. The dish would be irresistible.

Many of the servants, whether eligible for Social Security or not, performed hard physical labor in the vast homes day after day until they became too old or ill to put their shoulders to the grindstone. Many of the former servants were, in their later years, subsidized or supported by the oil family while living in their own meager homes.

After my acclimation to its scorching sun unsheltered by trees, I was neither intimidated or enamored of Big D. Missouri had seemed a conservative and sensible state during my childhood and teenage years, and I found Dallas' extravagances sometimes repulsive, but at other times, I was as amused as its natives.

As an experienced legal secretary, I easily obtained jobs listed in the newspaper, or through the aforementioned Texas employment service. I worked almost from the beginning for a socially accepted attorney whose deliberate efforts to establish his only daughter in the Dallas society register were almost embarrassing to witness. She "came out", was sent to France to study and learn the language, as well as social graces not indigenous to Dallas. Since I found her somewhat unattractive, and felt I knew how to judge a status I believed I shared, I followed her climb to the society pages with interest. All the while, I listened to her father complain of the cost. When my engagement was announced and I prepared to leave his employ, the attorney and his wife gave me a blanket as a wedding present. I felt the family found it difficult to select a gift that would fit my social status. Surely I would need comfort from the cold of Indiana.

When I became pregnant with our first child, Tom Watson and I returned to Dallas, where he practiced accounting and I became pregnant twice more. When almost frantic from homemaking, I would take secretarial jobs. In the longest stretch until Tom died at age 34 of a heart attack, I worked in the legal section of the Murchison Brothers company at 1201 Main. I was technically employed by the law firm of Jenkins, Anson and Spradley. Eight or more attorneys served the many businesses owned by the family but were controlled by strings held by Clint Jr, and John Dabney Murchison, sons of the fabulously wealthy Clint Murchison Sr. Clint Sr. and later his sons, were featured on the cover of Time magazine as icons of wealth and power.

I began to hear names almost daily that I had only read in newspapers–Great Southwest Corporation, Wynne, Jaffe and Tinsley, Sid Richardson, William McKenzie, and others. But only clothed in the context of business. The lawyers were closed-mouthed. I believed what I heard, that they were given tips to make money in stocks and real estate deals. It seemed a logical trade-off for the conditions under which they worked. They were highly stressed, somewhat like those described in John Grisham's, *The Firm*. I am not implying that anything illegal went on there. If it did, I never heard about it.

There were perks as an employee of the Murchisons, such as free home made cookies in the morning and a cafeteria lunch for the firm's employees only...well separated from the executive dining room.

The atmosphere in the building was of sheer fear–fear of displeasing the brothers. By that time, Clint, Sr. had left the building and was in stages of retirement, if not from spending money.

On one hot summer day the senior Murchison was brought in from his East Texas home to give a deposition. We secretaries lingered around the double doors of the 'law library', "listening in". The famous Texan, who was a close friend of Fort Worth oil billionaire Sid Richardson, was a crusty old codger who defiantly wore an open collared, white short sleeved shirt when he arrived to give his version of some legal dispute.

He gave his name in answer to attorneys' questions, but when asked his profession, he claimed to be a cattle breeder. Standing against the wall, I listened to the "pregnant pause" while attorneys sought the most tactful way to redirect the obstreperous entrepreneur. During the brief silence, old Clint leapt in with great gusto and began to describe what a cattle breeder does. (After all, the lawyers pause of disbelief might have been interpreted as a lack of understanding.) "Well, you take a bull into the barn..." he began, but several attorneys in concert cut short the description of the mating practices of cattle. Unfortunately, I quickly had to leave the show and return to my desk.

I remember that John Murchison would nod and grunt softly when passed in the hall, but Clint Jr. never acknowledged the "help" in any way. Jane Wolfe wrote in her book, *The Murchison*s, published in 1989, that Clint, Jr. was equally ill at ease in society. When greeted by an acquaintance at a party, Clint Jr. did not respond and was gently taken to task by a friend. Clint reportedly replied. "I saw him yesterday... How often do you have to speak to someone?"

Clint Sr. owned an island in Acuna with an airstrip and Clint Jr. later acquired one in the Caribbean. The oldest son also began building a 43,500 square foot house, in a horseshoe shape...the talk of Dallas.

Limestone was brought in by railroad car from Mexico to form the exterior. Wolfe reported that Clint, who planned every inch of the development, built an electronic system so lavish that even he was awed. Doors opened by touching buttons, a big screen television set slid from the ceiling on command, kitchen appliances glided into place, and of course each child had his or her own suite with living room and caregiver's quarters.

The planting of every tree was planned by Clint, after studying the proposed site and considering the impact of its foliage from every angle. A lighting system was installed in the trees and shrubbery.

The construction took years, while the family was cramped in a simple three bedroom house in north Dallas. Certainly more costly and spacious than my own, but hardly suitable for such a wealthy family. When even Clint could not deny that the new dwelling on Forest Lane was inhabitable, he agreed to move in one year. According to Wolfe, that time was just short of a decade after purchasing the property. He selected his fortieth birthday as the occasion. September 12 was scheduled for the debut of the home. The day was called "Christmas in September".

In Dallas, September usually spelled relief from temperatures in the upper nineties and above one hundred. It might have been as cool as 95° when workmen arrived with truckloads of artificial snow, which was generously scattered over the estate.

"Snow" covered trees and banked along the drive. Guests were dazzled as trees in one area glittered in the snow, then fell into darkness, and another area was illuminated.

The pool had a viewing window reached by a stairwell. Clint and Jane had a separate pool off their bedroom. Only glimpses of the structure could be seen from the street, but a friend of mine–naturally employed in construction–had seen it. He was most dazzled by the electronic "eye" which filled empty glasses with liquor when they were placed beneath. The home had a vast screen television as they were just being produced as prototypes. If an intruder ever dared to come too close to the home, he touched off an electronic invisible fortress, and became an instant prisoner.

At the office, I was for a time in charge of the Minute Book Room. Minutes of regular meetings of the corporations were inserted by me speedily and efficiently. I was told that dividends were declared at varied intervals, and stockholders would reinvest the proceeds in other Murchison holdings. Consequently little money ever left Murchison control. It was a tantalizing thought, even if inaccurate.

Writing about this aspect of Dallas concretely illustrates to me the difference in our classes. On my last Christmas in the Murchison attorneys' employ, the secretaries were to leave at noon on Christmas Eve to be with their families. However, on that year trust funds were created as Christmas presents for the grandchildren of Clint Sr. The project created an obstacle to the planned staff holiday. Stacks of paper covered the large table in the law library. Some paragraphs on the mutlti-page documents were identical but all were typed by the secretarial pool with many carbon copes. Others were individualized, and were carefully dictated by the attorneys. They were no happier that Christmas Eve than we, as we all labored until close to six p.m.

Documents and copies of documents, were bound. Our bosses stayed even later to assure delivery of the trust funds as Christmas presents to the grandchildren. We secretaries were neither thanked or acknowledged for our "slave labor". There was, of course, no overtime pay or bonuses. The turnover among secretaries was so frequent that after six months' tenure I became office manager.

When I became pregnant for the third and last time, and spent much of my time in the ladies room after eating the rich cafeteria food, I left and never considered returning to the fold.

Much more about his striking family is contained in Wolfe's book.

There are rich people everywhere, and the working classes. But it is my perception that in Dallas, at least in low-middle to middle class socio-economic families, the climb up the social ladder was especially active. Even in the area where the Watsons lived inside Northwest Highway, each new wife was asked what her husband "did". However banal his work, if his family was connected to any of Dallas' social class, the wives spent more on children's clothes and bought better furniture. "Keeping up with the Jones" was a game played by most.

On my own, I snooped around, sampling the city's cultural treats which were within economic reach, including the civic opera, lectures and museums. Of course, we visited Fair Park in nice weather to show visitors the Cotton Bowl and the site of the "largest state fair in the United States". Even that fact may have been the product of public relations, although it has been written as fact. But like other Dallasites, I assumed that if it was in Dallas, it was the largest ever.

A neighbor and her husband were members of the John Birch Society, and cordially invited me to a cell meeting. I went, just once, and found the members to be more diverse than I had expected.

Literature warning of Communist dangers were crudely printed and available in great quantity. Some members were couples similar to my neighbors. The "man of the family" was a West Point graduate, firmly ensconced in the belief that a strong military force was essential to our freedom. Others at the meeting were quiet, secretive men who seemed to my layman's mind, paranoid in their view of the threat. General Edwin Walker was a hero to them. I saw no guns, but literature did laud the virtues of certain weaponry over others. I liked this family, but had no interest in the John Birch Society. I believe that I can see the city objectively from my frame of reference. I know that the President could have been killed anywhere, but there was no more politically syntonic setting than Dallas in 1963, or even earlier in the ten years I had lived in the city.

As a lay person, I would be uncomfortable writing such a statement without support. Warren Leslie was an Easterner turned Dallasite. He had been a reporter with the *Dallas Morning News*. Quickly, he and his wife began to move with the elite as patrons of the arts, through an obvious affinity with the interests of the upper class. Leslie was the author of the most definitive book I ever read about the city, *Dallas, Public and Private*, published in 1964. Leslie quoted Professor Reese McGee, head of the sociology department at the University of Texas, writing in a national publication: "Barring the probability of Mississippi, in a doomed and fated way it had to be in Texas, and in Texas, Dallas."[4]

Thinking of the strange political aura which surrounded Dallas, facts unlikely to exist in any other American city must be considered.

Leslie wrote that "Dallas is run by a group which has no mandate from the people and which is not subject to recall".[5] But interestingly, he seemed to contradict himself when he wrote: "Dallas is a business city, especially a financial center, and its dollar power allies it closely to Wall Street."[6]

I will explore the details of Dallas later in order not to disrupt the chain of Leslie's interesting observations. He went on to say that Dallas "is not run by a power elite of two hundred; it is run–or strongly led–by a group of at most ten, at fewest three, men". Leslie cited such familiar names as Robert Cullum, J. Erik Jonsson and James Ling, and wrote: "If these nine men agree on something, and if at the same time the newspapers, led by Joe Dealey (the News) and James Chambers (the Times-Herald) also agree, this automatically means that the two Dallas television stations will agree, since they are owned by the newspapers." That group assured that the rest of the city would follow. He termed it government by a private club, hence government by junta.[7]

While the Mayoralty was an elected position in the 60's, it was not always so. When Earle Cabell retired to run for congress, five Councilmen, controlled by the Citizens' Charter Association, a wing of the Citizens' Council, asked Erik Jonsson to accept the job, and Jonsson did. According to Leslie, Larry Kelly, executive director of the Dallas Civic Opera, laughed about the feat and reportedly said, "I think we have the only city in the world where it could happen."[8] Exactly.

An article published in Fortune Magazine in 1949 proclaimed: "...Everything in Dallas is bigger and better, the parties are plusher, the buildings are more air-conditioned, the women better dressed and the girls more fetching. And in all of these things, it is finally a monument to sheer determination. Dallas doesn't owe a thing to accident, nature or inevitability. It is what it is–even to the girls–because the men of Dallas damned well planned it that way."[9]

To Leslie, the oligarchy were the "working" members of the Council. The oil men weren't the same. They simply 'were'; they were too wealthy to be corralled when work time came; they lived where they wanted to live. Here, I dare to disagree. Many of those men, or at least their fathers, had toiled in the mud and built towers on red clay, time after time defeating the threatening dry hole and bringing in a gusher. They worked, but at a different level than other CEOs. Clint Murchison, Jr. changed the face of the city when he built Texas Stadium. The difference was, he didn't have to ask anyone's permission. H.L. Hunt didn't lift a hand to operate a radio program, "Life Line". Yet that radio program helped immeasurably to create the hotbed in which radical thinking flourished.

Some of the values were "wild western" and some Southern. Leslie claimed there were an inordinate number of rifles and handguns, a fact supported by a prize winning newspaper series written by two fellow reporters at the *Dallas Times Herald*. The stories focused on the rising crime in Dallas in 1964.

In truth, many were concerned about Kennedy visiting Dallas. The reasons centered on the political arena noted herein. William Manchester, acclaimed author of *The Death of a President*, quoted Stanley Marcus, civic leader and owner of the famous Neiman-Marcus department store, as saying that he believed he and other Dallas leaders should "talk him out of it". Marcus reportedly told his top executives, "I don't think this city is safe for it". Marcus shared vague fears about the tempestuous actions of some Dallas citizens in regard to politics.

"The Mayor asked the city to redeem itself and shed its reputation as the 'Southwest hate capital of Dixie,' again claimed Manchester.

Said Manchester, There was a chorus of warnings. And then there was a catastrophe. Between the two lies an abyss which can be adequately explored–

> Between the idea...
> And the reality...
> Falls the shadow."[10]

Dallas, in 1963, could hardly be considered an anarchistic society threatening the free world. It was though, a political anomaly. After all, visitors to the city for the first time were sometimes startled to be greeted by a mammoth billboard on the side of the highway with gigantic letters spelling "WELCOME TO DALLAS. THE HOME OF THE JOHN BIRCH SOCIETY".

Nineteen

Walker, To Alger, To Cabell

General Edwin Walker, had been relieved of his command of a division of the U.S. Army in 1961 for distributing right wing literature to his troops. (The Assassination of John F. Kennedy; Dates. Places. People, p. 481.) Walker was a Dallas citizen, living on lavish Turtle Creek Boulevard in a house that appears, through photographs, to have needed attention.

Granted, he was a busy man. Walker made many appearances throughout the country, endorsing right wing issues. While such actions were common to many Americans, General Walker carried them to the extreme typical of Dallas.

Under the letterhead, "Edwin A. Walker" he sent out a form letter to thousands of American citizens. Reprinted here, it displays Walker at his mildest.

"Dear Friend:

Thank you for your expression of interest. National concern for the survival of our traditions and heritage is reflected in letters I have received (four thousand before I left Germany), and continue to receive. These, with over 150 invitations to speak across the nation – not counting the demand for appearances since my filing for Governor of Texas – place me under obligation to people in practically every State in the Union. It was an inspiration to me to appear before great audiences in Dallas, Jackson, Amarillo, Los

Angeles, Odessa, and Chicago, totaling 35,000, with an estimated additional 30 million listeners and viewers over radio and television.

My pending appearance before the Special Preparedness Subcommittee under Senator John C. Stennis of Mississippi is also an important obligation to all Americans. I have been invited to attend, and have accepted. The appearance is being continually delayed.

In the Governor's race my platform and campaign are unique. My stand for Constitutional rights and States Rights is unmatched by any other candidate – as is my demand for national security. This strict Constitutionalism, which is our greatest defense and offense, has given me the most extensive grass-roots support and aroused much national interest.

Support of my campaign has broken and re-formed many lines and barriers. I am fighting in and through the party of Jefferson, where the greatest number of Texas patriots can express themselves on the basic and vital issue of national survival, and where we can meet head-on opponents of the Jeffersonian States Rights tradition.

Extensive offers of assistance have come in, even from beyond the borders of Texas. I am appealing for the support of nine million free and independent Texans. I am free and independent myself, and will remain so I am financed by no one individual or group of individuals. I hope for the support of all. Those who desire to support our cause are asked to work for votes and for campaign funds. People throughout the nation can help, with influence, contacts, and letters to friends and the press. I sincerely appreciate the response of all – particularly of the many in Texas who are now working hard in support of my campaign.

Information necessary for our people to make right decisions includes knowledge of the planned program for our disarmament, as given in State Department Publication 7277, entitled "Freedom from War." All Americans should be made familiar with this shocking plan to place all our armed forces and all our weapons in an international army under the UN, except what may be necessary for internal police. I ask: Who is to de-Americanize our soldiers and UN-ize them for this service? How, under the oath of office, can any U. S. official or officer train our soldiers to man weapons which may be fired against this country on UN decision? If we permit the provisions of State Department Publication 7277 to be carried out, it means the end of this nation. I sincerely hope and pray that our people are given the necessary information in time to prevent this catastrophe.

The danger is not confined to what is usually thought of as the national level. The people should know that 323 times in the past year legislation has been attempted at some level of government to abridge their Constitutional right to have and hold personal private firearms. These attempted laws included various means and methods of control, registration, or limitation of firearms.

It should not be overlooked that laws depriving our citizens of the right to bear arms not only violate Amendment II of the U. S. Constitution, but also constitute psychological preparation for the surrender of the means of national defense, as outlined in Publication 7277. The interpretation of "weapons" in this publication can include private firearms. My vital concern for the preservation of Constitutional liberty and American independence is what has compelled me to seek a public office where I can act to carry out the mandate of nine million free Texans.

My apologies that this must be a form letter. I could not possibly write at length to so many individuals, and a brief note would not be at all adequate to express my appreciation of your serious concern for the state of the nation. My earnest thanks for the understanding and great support I am receiving in Texas, and from my many friends in 49 other States. Through the guidance and grace of God we will perpetuate our liberty, and extend our freedom to all mankind.

With gratitude and respect, I am

Sincerely yours,

Edwin A. Walker

Granted, the foregoing letter is hardly stronger than some right wing extremist stances taken in Congress today, but we must look further for Walker's inner quest. He sent U.S. Congressman Bruce Alger, Dallas representative, a printed card quoting from an address before the Lenin School of Political Warfare in Moscow in 1931 by Dimity Z. Msnuilsky. Quoting Walker, he calls Msnuilsky a Soviet official and at one time the presiding officer of the UN Security Council.

The quote:
"War to the hilt between Communism and Capitalism is inevitable...As soon as their guard is down, we shall smash them with our clenched fist."

Printed at the bottom of the card is the message: "This is the enemy, who preaches coexistence like a wolf in sheep's clothing. Your representatives in Washington, who have failed, and are failing, to recognize this, must be replaced. N.A.L. (Please give this to a friend)"

Walker sought the friendship of Congressman Alger, saying he was Alger's friend. Alger, however, was a politician and no idiot. He did not endorse Walker's platform or approach. In a long platform statement, Walker pledged to stand on the Constitution, regard the "Governor of Texas" a national position, ward off the dangers of Communism, fight aid to Cuba, and finally described the evils of World Communism. His concluding point is printed verbatim:

"U S. Defense Pivots on Texas
And if there is a region of the United States which more than any other must be vigilant to prevent a paralyzing pincers movement of assault from without and subversion from within, it is the whole Southern tier of States of which Texas is the pivot. The proximity of Latin America, where false propaganda against "Yankee imperialism" has made headway (helped by policies of recent Administrations in Washington); the location of most of the major military, naval, air, and atomic installations of the country; and the presence of racial situations which are actually a source of unique cultural benefits, here and world-wide, but which Communists traditionally regard as an area for destructive exploitation - all these factors combine to make Texas a prime target of Soviet attention.

At the same time, the tradition of Texas, to fear God and nobody else, to love our homes and fight for our rights - the tradition of the Alamo and San Jacinto - means that Texas is a bulwark against Communism, both for herself and for the whole United States.

Three Points

Again I pledge my life with God's help to
NATIONAL SECURITY
STATES RIGHTS, and
INDIVIDUAL LIBERTY

I ask you to support me, and the Sovereign State of Texas, with your prayers your efforts, and your votes.

Edwin A. Walker
w-4"

Walker reportedly had a large female following, which I can neither prove nor disprove. It is apparent that Dallas' women generally stood right of center–even in their support of Congressman Alger.

One letter sent by the John Birch Society apparently hit a nerve when received by Fred Hardin. Hardin wrote to Alger, under the letterhead of the Proctor & Gamble Manufacturing Company in Dallas, a letter of criticism. The letter was not necessarily the work of Walker, but certainly supported his views. Hardin wrote to Congressman Alger:

"THE PROCTER & GAMBLE MANUFACTURING COMPANY

5530 Columbia Ave.
Dallas 14, Texas.
April 19,1961.

Hon. Bruce Alger,
Washington, D.C.

Dear Mr. Alger

I was recently handed a letter originated by The John Birch society in which I was requested to write you asking your aid in impeaching Earl Warren of The Supreme Court. Instead I am asking that you call for some sort of investigation of this society. From all that I can find out I believe their action subversive and a threat to free society. I was approached in much the same manner regarding The KKK several years ago. This John Birch outfit seem to me to be a cross between Fascist, Nazi and communist. It is true that I have regretted some of the decisions of the Supreme Court but I have felt that they followed closely the Constitution. Consequently Mr. Warren has been rather honest in most decisions. Mr. Welsh might well add his charges against Eisenhower and other fine men, all the framers of The Constitution and also Jesus Christ. Any man so irresponsible as Welsh has been should be investigated. In view of increasing following by what I have always called "JOINERS" this group could well become a dangerous element in our government and our society.

Very Truly Yours,

Fred Hardin"

Alger, in turn, used unusual caution in regard to General Walker. When Walker decided to run for governor of the State of Texas, a headline in the Dallas Morning News said: "Alger to Oppose Walker Strongly".

Alger so surprised the conservative newspaper that the story, bylined by Mike Quinn, began this way:

Remember the old radio show 'Who Said That?' –where the announcer would read a statement and the panel would guess who said it?

"Well, try this one:

'I will oppose General Walker just as completely as I can...'

"If you've been guessing names on the far left of some middle-of-the-roaders, you are way off."

"This was right-wing Dallas Republican Congressman Bruce Alger's reply to a question about Edwin A. Walker's decision to run for governor of Texas as a Democrat...''

Whether an elected official only mirrors the opinions of the majority of his constituents, or whether he can influence his voters by independent action is a question without an answer. Perhaps there can be such a thing as a mental marriage between a block of voters and the man they elected. Bruce Alger certainly had more than supporters. He had a following.

In 1961, he divorced his wife and the mother of his children in a highly publicized court hearing. Strangely, the news stories, especially those carried in the *Dallas Morning News*, were seemingly acceptable, almost understanding. Mrs. Alger said that their trouble centered around his contention that she was intellectually unworthy of being the wife of a Princeton graduate.

She believed that he placed his political career above his family, and claimed that he had stated so. Furthermore, she believed the administration had ceased "grooming him" as a Vice Presidential candidate because of her lack of suitability as a Vice President's wife. In a news story, the reporter noted that at one time during the testimony, Mrs. Alger was seen to cross the courtroom and speak to her husband. A property settlement had seemed to be reached. One can only wonder why Mrs. Alger did not defend herself for meeting the intellectual reasoning a rabid radical politician.

A headline in the Dallas Morning News on September 1962, claimed: Bruce Alger Urges Cuba Blockade Now. The article, written by Kent Biffle, began:

> "Republican Congressman Bruce Alger, seeking re-election in November, lashed out at the Kennedy Administration and called for an immediate U.S. blockade of Cuba in a talk before 4,500 here Saturday night."

Biffle went on to say that the barbecue was held in Alger's honor at the Dallas-Garland Airport. (As a former Dallasite, I call that a good sized party even for Big D.)

Of course, Alger wisecracked, "This meeting tonight is non-political... just like the President's trip west." It seems that politicians never need new jokes—the same old 'saws' get press attention.

Defending his call for the economic blockade, Alger reportedly said, "There's risk involved. There's risk in any military operation. But the risk will be greater later. And it's not too late now."

It is perfectly clear that Alger did not like the Kennedys, Jack or Bobby. He also seemed to believe he was what the country needed. A small story carried in the Times Herald on June 23, 1963, reported: Alger Seen As Good President. The story read: U.S. Rep. Bruce Alger, R-Tex., of Dallas, was mentioned Saturday as a member of the GOP who would make "a good President," according to former U.S. Rep John Rousselot, R-Calif. If the reader should not recognize Rousselot, the article said he was "in charge of the John Birch operations in six western states".

In another news article headlined: Alger Charges Kennedy Plans Freedom Curb, it was reported that Alger charged that President Kennedy was asking "that the people of the United States surrender their freedom". After claiming that Kennedy sought a society which would abolish individual enterprise, he was reported to say, "For the initiative of the people he (Kennedy) would substitute a hierarchy of bureaucrats who would–as all-wise patriarchs–make all the decisions, direct the lives of all the people, promise cradle to grave security and ask only in return that the people surrender their freedom".

He also said the President had "an almost complete record of failure" as chief executive, and had moved the country "very close to the rule of a dictatorship".

Representative Alger also considered atheism unlawful, again according to news reports. To a Christian audience, the flamboyant official reminded his audience that almost every fundamental document upon which the nation's laws are based contain "in clear and forthright language the concept that belief in God is basic to our government".

He went on to say, "It follows then, without equivocation, that in the United States of America, it is unlawful to be an atheist." It would appear that Alger believed he could create laws without support of precedent.

In Washington, he inserted into the Congressional Record a statement that "Administration officials are trying to sell the U.S. a policy that bears the brushmarks of Communist conspirators".

Fearing that the reader might ask me where I am going with this history, I say that when readers are told that Dallasites were, in part, radical thinkers, there is reason for that accusation. I quote one article in some detail. It was filed (according to a handwritten notation at the Dallas public library) by the Washington Bureau of the *Dallas Times Herald* on July 12, 1963. The headline reads:

Alger Says JFK Acts as Dictator.

"Dallas Congressman Bruce Alger Friday accused President Kennedy of substituting his will for that of Congress and, in effect, of assuming the role of dictator.

Alger fired his salvo against the White House in a speech before the Political Action Conference, sponsored by the right-wing magazine "Human Events".

'President Kennedy is operating as chief executive without regard to the rule of law,' Alger charged.

'The most blatant use of presidential force was his action against the steel industry last year wherein he dictated prices with no legal authority and without any type of congressional action.'

The congressman also attacked the President's 'illegal' settlement of the East Coast dock strike earlier in the year, his trade expansion bill of 1962, and his actions involving proposed rail and airline mergers."

"Do his actions represent lack of knowledge concerning the motivation of people and the operation of a private enterprise system, or are they deliberate because the President feels, in fact, that he already is acting in the role of a dictator without responsibility to either Congress or the people," Alger asked.

The article printed an abbreviated version of Alger's own program which would include getting the government out of business, putting labor under anti-trust laws and other measures.

The magnitude of Alger's weight in the city of Dallas and the rightist slant is shown by a few headlines from Dallas papers, all calling public attention to his views. A sampling includes: "Alger to Continue Attack on Kennedy", "Communists Pulling for Dems, Alger Says", "Alger Batters JFK, Foes Hit Incumbent", "R. Kennedy Libels Dallas, Alger Says", "Alger Lists 10 'Trampled' Civil Rights" and "Alger Defends City, Condemns UN." In the last article the Congressman defended Dallasites for their attack on UN Ambassador Adlai Stevenson. After stating that he did not condone the act, he said that people "become intemperate" (an admission that they allowed emotion to become physical acts) but added that "such things" (UN actions) should not prohibit them from speaking out.

By June 4, 1964, Mayor Earle Cabell resigned to run for Congress against Alger. His victory indicated that the majority of Dallas citizens', or those with the most power, were losing their patience with the unbridled venom of Bruce Alger. Cabell lamented the diminished chance of Dallas receiving a "Trinity Canal", and blamed the set-back on Alger. In an article in the News, Cabell said that Alger had turned other Congressmen against him. Cabell pointed out that the Dallas federal center was included in the 1960 budget and then vetoed by Republican President Eisenhower. Cabell charged that Alger congratulated the President on his action. Cabell was reported to have termed the action "another example of Alger's inconsistency".

If we Dallasites had known that there was a man with little money, a man named Lee Harvey Oswald living in Irving, and that he had lived in the Soviet Union for two and a half years, we would hardly have been concerned. We had enough on our minds to sort out the truth as defined by Alger, the Birchers and the few extremely mild Democrats who said the rest of the country was just uninformed. Dallasites, after all, did more and knew more. Irving, Grand Prairie and such peripheral towns were mere "hick towns" where no one of importance lived. Fort Worth was called "cow town", and Oak Cliff was the wrong side of the Dallas tracks. Persons of "no importance" did not do important things. In my opinion, Alger was wrong. But living in the climate of extremes made me immune to tones of temperance. There seemed no way to make conclusive judgments. I was relatively young in the early sixties, but I blame myself–as one voter among many–who felt that there was little we could do to change the status quo in Dallas, except to vote. Such acts of omission contributed, in my belief, to perpetuation of a deadly political setting.

Twenty

Deep D

Author Peter Dale Scott jars a student of the assassination toward the face of reality. After reading his book, *Deep Politics and the Death of JFK*, I wonder if Marina Oswald took a single independent step in the year following her husband's death. Her earliest testimony was distorted in translation by Peter Gregory, who took even more steps leading to her control. Gregory's distortion in regard to the description of Oswald's rifle, Scott contends, "to supply the baseless story already reported by Gregory's friend Mamantov, of Oswald's 'dark and scopeless' rifle".[11] The discrepancies, while few, changed her description of an ordinary rifle to the description in the quoted sentence.

Scott describes how Gregory "assumed responsibility for delivering Marina into the hands of the Great Southwest Corporation, a real estate venture controlled in Dallas by the wealthy family of Bedford Wynne."[12]

James Herbert Martin, a Great Southwest employee, became Marina's first manager. When he was fired, William A. McKenzie, a lawyer from the Wynne family (which represented Great Southwest) became Marina's lawyer. Scott writes, "Both men, along with other employees of Great Southwest, were responsible for highly questionable 'links' between powerful Murchison oil and construction interests in Texas..."[13]

Further, Bedford Wynne was the subject of a critical audit regarding his "salary" from Sweetwater Development which Scott says was set up by the Murchison's Tecon Corporation through the firm of Wynne, Jaffe, and Tinsley.[14]

Wynne was also part of the "Bobby Baker set" in Washington, Scott relates. Seemingly greatly respected civic leaders were not just interested in running Dallas; they instead were part of a hierarchy reaching upward to associates of elected officials and the administrative branch of the government.

Ignored by the Warren Commission was how Peter Gregory had the power to make phone calls which led to Marina's stay at the Great Southwest hotel. Also unasked is how Gregory was selected as Marina's interpreter on November 23.[15]

Marina would certainly not have questioned Gregory, as she already knew him. But was this acquaintanceship innocently made? I dare not make an assumption.

The Warren Commission, Scott notes, did not report the existence of William McKenzie's new telephone number (RI 1-1295) in the notebook of Larry Craford, Jack Ruby assistant.[16]

Craford also, some thought, resembled Oswald. There were several Oswald "lookalikes" in Dallas. One worked for a Dallas businessman who reportedly lived on the same street as Tippit. The latter lookalike reportedly "roped" some local cowboys into a rodeo scheme in which he was to import a fighting Mexican bull. When the lookalike failed to fulfill his responsibility, he left town. When I questioned my interviewee–the son of the businessman–about what happened to the scam artist, he just grinned and said, "I know what would have happened if those cowboys had caught up with him."

Also reportedly in Craford's notebook was the name of Pete White, a former district attorney, who got a pistol-carrying charge dismissed against Jack Ruby. White also "ran into" Ruby on November 20, 1964.[17]

Larrie Schmidt, often written about as a out-of-Dallas entrepreneur who helped originate the black-bordered ad which appeared in the *Dallas Morning News* on November 22, had help from General Edwin Walker, who could hardly have been unknown to any Dallasite. The only person in Schmidt's group who was indicted on criminal charges related to the ad was Robert Hatfield. He hired Pete White to represent him. Schmidt's cabal, CUSA (Conservatism, USA) included the local chapter of the right-wing Young Americans for Freedom, including Warren Carroll, described by Schmidt as a "scriptwriter for H.L. Hunt".[18]

I wish to quote directly from Deep Politics: "We learn there that Schmidt's CUSA member in charge of public relations, Art Fraznszwald, was at the 'Bedford Wynne PR agency'(18 WH 879).

This indicates that CUSA had not only conspicuous links to the extreme right-wingers like Morris and the Hunts but also more secretive links to the 'center' world of the Wynne's and their Murchison and Rockefeller allies (as embodied in the Great Southwest Corporation)."[19]

Power of the Press

Warren Leslie, author of Dallas Public and Private, (see chapter 18) was careful to add the weight carried by Dealey and Chambers of the News and the Herald respectively to the ruling class of Dallas. He was acutely aware of the power of the press. But such power must never be interpreted to mean the power of reporters or television newsmen.

Publishers sit on special thrones in city government, as Leslie noted. Seldom are they such opposing forces some consider them to be. If resistance to compromise arises, one will probably financially succumb. The lowest of reporters knew, even in 1963, that publishers were the guardians of the establishment. In many instances the editors would meet and decide which side each would cover on an given issue. Thus any major dispute would be neutralized...just as in marriages when husbands and wives march to the polls to cancel out the other's vote.

At the time of this writing, as most cities have only one newspaper, it is even simpler. The flick of a television remote gives the viewer a slightly different view of a limited version of the same story. From an honest anchor man, I once heard that the television media takes advantage of the swiftness of seconds to skew the facts. After all, the television short story is quickly forgotten. Not so for the print media. A worn newspaper story may always be hauled out to check its veracity.

The tentacles of "tolerated" or "organized" crime undoubtedly extended throughout the press. The wire service war in 1946-47 was indicative of the role of the politics of crime. Rufus King, described as a gambling authority, said: "To attribute half the gang killings and mob violence of the forties to battles over control of this gambling empire would be very conservative explanation. Whoever controlled the wire service 'drops' in a town became master of gambling activities there..."[20]

As late as early 1970, while managing a book store, an owner of a successful newsstand told me the "syndicate" controlled his business.

Peter Dale Scott called organized crime "tolerated crime; it is the milieu which private and government interests have turned when there was fraud, violence or murder to be done." Yet crime must also be characterized as utilized, as well as tolerated. It does not play a passive role. Bobby Gene Moore, an employee of Civello's importing company, was also a piano player for Ruby. Moore said "Ruby was a frequent visitor at Civello's store and an associate of Civello. Blakey also concluded that Ruby knew Civello's deputy Joe Campisi–a fame familiar even to this writer while in Dallas.[21]

While Blakey focused narrowly on organized crime as a possible body responsible for the assassination, it certainly cannot be eliminated by any rational student. Civello attended the famous 1957 meeting, called the Appalachian meeting, which embarrassed J. Edgar Hoover, who had taken the public stance that organized crime was not of importance in the United States.

Rather than belabor the issue of the importance of organized crime in Dallas, it must be admitted it was there, live and well. Then we must examine what was its purpose to the "administrators" of Dallas–a large group including the Dallas Police, local military intelligence and upward to the oil wealthy. Lt. Jack Revill, who helped drive the search which turned up the Carcano on the sixth floor of the TSBD, reportedly knew an Army Intelligence agent who was also present on the sixth floor. Revill stated: "Whether or not Jack Ruby was used as a source of information (to narcotics investigators), and there is a difference, this I don't know."[22] Peter Dale Scott reminds us that Revill himself told the commission that he had known Ruby since 1953; Vice Squad Detective Richard L. Clark reported that he "contacted Ruby on investigative matters on an average of once a month."[23]

If organized crime is connected to police activities, and few are so naive as to think it is not, at least on some occasions and at some times. It would be even more ignorant to think that Dallas' oil rich did not utilize its services when required. The Teamsters' Pension Fund investments were placed with the Murchisons, Irving Davidson, their lobbyist, and the mob in Las Vegas.[24] Money from the Teamsters went to Webb and Knapp, keeping it alive in 1963, and much of that capital was tied up in a joint Yankee-cowboy Dallas-Fort Worth real estate venture... The investment was in the Great Southwest Corporation, where control centered in the Rockefeller and Wynne families. House Committee on Banking and Currency, Penn Central Failure Report, III, 30. This report also reveals that John J. McCloy, chairman of the Rockefeller-dominated Chase Manhattan Bank, became a financial ally of Clint Murchison Sr, and his best friend, Sid Richardson. The woven web extends too far to be controlled. Example: Warren Commission assistant counsel Francis H. Adams represented the Murchisons in 1959 in the conflict over Allegheny Corporation.

A perhaps lethal layer active in Dallas was the military. Author Scott contends that along with Deputy Police Chief Lumpkin in the pilot car of the motorcade was a member of the Army Intelligence Reserve, and also the local army reserve commander as an unscheduled occupant.[25] Army intelligence agent James W. Powell was nearby when a man had an epileptic seizure (invalidated). Special agent Powell was soon trapped in the TSBD after the doors were sealed.[26]

To think of Jack Ruby as a "force of power" in Dallas would seem to give unwarranted importance to a disorganized, perverted, often financially needy individual. However, one must separate the personality of the man from the role he played. Ruby, associated to the Mafia, called "La Cosa Nostra" in new York City, had well placed connections in crime. Reportedly, Joseph Civello took over the Mafia in Dallas in 1956.

In the early 1960's, the newspapers were the ruling media power. Yet it is ironic that one of the most impactful television stories to reach the American public occurred within 36 hours after the President was killed–the "live" story of the homicide of Lee Oswald, the President's alleged assassin. It, of course, also occurred in Dallas.

The microcosm called "Big D" shifted slightly as it again became biggest and first, but certainly not best. Not this time; especially not this time. Considerable embarrassment surrounded the killing of Oswald in the police basement, and even led to an independent investigation and the eventual fall from power of Police Chief Jesse Curry.

Still, by most citizens, Ruby's action was shrugged off as typical of him, and according to Chief Curry, probably fated to happen. Few police officers knew Ruby, Curry insisted, in the only book he published, *JFK Assassination File*. Actually most people, and definitely those on Curry's force, knew that many officers knew Ruby. This very interesting commentary is now out of print. Such statements are typical of his attempt to save what shred of respectability he could for the Dallas Police Force. But he also included several statements worthy of critics' note.

If one lets such complicated and yet telling information sink in, imagine the feelings of the Warren Commission meeting in executive session on January 22, 1964. Quoting Peter Dale Scott, "The sensational development (Warren Council) Rankin explained, was the claim of Attorney General Waggoner Carr of Texas that Lee Harvey Oswald had been a paid FBI informant." The (commission) was stunned. "If that was true and it ever came out and could be established," Rankin said, "then you have people thinking that there was a conspiracy to accomplish this assassination that nothing the Commission did or anybody could dissipate."

BOGGS: You are right.
DULLES: Oh, terrible.
BOGGS: The implications of this are fantastic, don't you think so?
WARREN: Terrific.
RANKIN: Now it is something that will be very difficult to prove out...I am confident that the FBI will never admit it, and I presume their records will never show it.

> Transcript of Warren Commission
> executive session, January 22, 1964,
> quoted by Curt Gentry in J. Edgar
> Hoover

Craig Roberts, author of *Kill Zone* and several other books, gives views I have never read before. With his permission, I quote part of two chapters which directly relate to Dallas.

"It has been said that money is power. This is true. But when history is examined it can be determined that the majority of the world's monetary assets fall into the hands of a few privileged families and the banks and businesses they control. The names of these families are not secret; they are the social elite of Europe and America that have controlled the destiny of nations for over two hundred years. Only by understanding where world power really emanates can we understand exactly who makes up the power behind the throne of not only the United States, but every modern country in the world today.

The normal progression after attending university is Wall Street. Here, the young elitist either goes into law, as did John J. McCloy, Allen Dulles, John Foster Dulles, and John Mitchell, or into an international investment bank such as Chase Manhattan. Ultimately, he or she may work in both institutions. In any case, those that follow the family ties normally serve a stint in government, typically as a cabinet member, Senator, or administration head. Others may end up in "think tanks" like the Rand Corporation or the Brookings Institute. Many will eventually serve on the boards of such institutions as the Ford, Carnegie or Rockefeller foundations. And a privileged few will enter the Oval Office as President of the United States.

But no matter what career path they follow, no matter who they are or what family they come from, there is a prerequisite for success: membership in the Council on Foreign Relations.

Since its founding in 1921, the Council on Foreign Relations, or CFR, has been the chief link between the eastern money powers and the federal government. Virtually every president was surrounded by members of the CFR, and almost every president since that year has been a member.

The Council, which serves efficiently as a front organization for the Establishment and a clandestine contact point between U. S. government officials and foreign powers, has been called "The heart of the American Establishment." Within its membership rolls are such names as Rockefeller, Morgan, Peabody, Stimson, McCloy, Dulles, Harriman, Vanderbilt, Nixon, Kissinger, Carter, Oppenheimer, Westmoreland, McNamara, Bush and Clinton.

Only by linking together the players and the organizations involved in the stories told on these pages can one see the continuity of people and events. Multitudes of men like John J. McCloy, Averill Harriman, and Henry Kissinger, all of whom held more positions of power in their political careers than did virtually any president of the United States, seemed to lurk in the background ever since the Revolution. But few have been previously exposed for what they really were: agents of the Power Elite and pawns in the Rothschild Plan. Even during the administration of John F. Kennedy, who was the only president since 1921 who refused membership in the inner circle when offered, the cabinet was filled with representatives of the conspirators. There is little room for maneuvering when one is surrounded by the enemy.

Many motives have been offered through the years for the death of John F. Kennedy. A few, upon study, are valid up to a point. Of these, there are:

1. The anti-Castro Cubans, who, assisted by former CIA controllers, avenged the Bay of Pigs debacle;

2. The CIA, who if Kennedy was eliminated, would remain intact instead of being "scattered to the winds" as Kennedy threatened;

3. The Mafia, who wished to "get rid of the Kennedy boys" who were causing them so many problems, and finally,

4. The Military/Industrial/Banking complex that stood so much to gain from the escalating war in Vietnam - from which Kennedy had announced the U.S. was withdrawing.

5. Lyndon Johnson and his Texas backers who had so much to gain from the War in Vietnam and the power the presidency brings."

But even though the plot would, to a certain extent, require the cooperation of selected elements of each of these entities, the most important motive is not on this list.

"Kennedy's death could not be attributed solely to the Cubans, the CIA, the Mafia, or the M/I/B complex. Instead, the reason behind the decision to eliminate the president was something far more important to the conspirators than revenge or war profits: President John F. Kennedy, like Lincoln before him, was about to interfere with the progress of the master plan. After two hundred years of alternating victories and setbacks for the international banking cabal, and just when they had total power within their grasp by way of controlling the nation's economy, Kennedy planned to exterminate the Federal Reserve System, then put the country back on the Gold Standard. In this action he would put the country back on a cash-and-carry basis, get away from deficit spending, and eventually eliminate the national debt-as had Andrew Jackson and Abraham Lincoln before him when they did the same to the two Rothschild-organized central banks!"

I am not endorsing the "scope" of the aforementioned thinking, but Mr. Roberts reminds us that Dallas did not exist in a vacuum.

I do subscribe to the theory of high power government instigation. Was the National Security Council consulted in the assassination of JFK, or did the order issue from it to other interested groups? The highest of powers must have known...they must also have approved.

PART V

DEPENDENT CONCLUSIONS

Men fear thought as they fear nothing else on earth—more than death. Thought is subversive, and revolutionary, destructive and terrible; thought is merciless to privilege, established institutions, and comfortable habits; thought is anarchic and lawless, indifferent to authority, careless to the well-tried wisdom of the ages. Thought looks into the pit of hell and is not afraid...Thought is great and swift and free, the light of the world, and the chief glory of man.

But if thought is to become the possession of the many, and not the privilege of the few, we must have done with fear. It is fear that holds men back—fear that their cherished beliefs should prove delusions, fear lest the institutions by which they live should prove harmful, fear lest they themselves prove less worthy to the respect than they have supposed themselves to be.

Bertrand Russell (Lord Russell)
British mathematician philosopher

Twenty One

The Researchers

In the early years after the assassination of President John F. Kennedy, researchers were as varied in intent and approach as their personalities. They were breaking ground; strong wills naturally accompanied their work.

Reviewing the personality characteristics of Mark Lane, Sylvia Meagher and Harold Weisberg is a case in point. Lane enjoyed the spotlight and formed some opinions based on "gut reactions". He wrote prolifically, and had first hand experiences with the Warren Commission. Meagher was at least publicly known for her independence. Obviously highly intelligent, Meagher was caustic in her approach to her book, *Accessories After The Fact*. Taking a pot shot at someone she believed had been sloppy in his or her job was not above Meagher. Even if she was wrong. (See Appendix B) Weisberg was and is outspoken and vehemently indignant. When information was withheld he put his attorney on the case. He won several law suits based on the freedom of information laws. He has not changed to this day. Yet the three researchers mentioned had one characteristic in common: They all did copious research through collection of interviews, newspaper reports, evidence and personal observation.

While many fine researchers are still at work on the Kennedy assassination project, some research has been contaminated. Such viruses have entered the body of work by the competition of researchers to supply something new year after year, which brought about the adoption of others' work as their own. Some occurs innocently. Some, not all, study other researcher's work, find it compatible with their own findings and then supplement their writing by adding conclusions drawn by others. Unfortunately, less scrupulous writers and researchers have adopted previously published work as their own. Some of the points made in this section were first published in a booklet entitled *"For the Defense"* co-authored myself and an experienced, established researcher who now prefers to be anonymous. Such practices cause the eager virus to spread, diluting the importance of areas of study. Further, writers who call themselves researchers distort, even lie, about credible testimony and evidence, damaging the body of work without hesitation. Their motives are simple. They have a great deal of money invested in the status quo of the "American system"–governmental and capitalism–and under the guise of "patriotism", they seek to destroy. An early researcher said that she broke off contact with another group of researchers when, to her dismay, she discovered they were merely right wing radicals intent on establishing Lee Oswald was a Communist.

Hence, I have chosen to call this part of *Secrets from the Sixth Floor Window* "Dependent Conclusions" because firstly, I am not qualified to be a researcher and reach an independent conclusion, nor do I chose to be a researcher, and secondly, my conclusions are based on experiences I had thirty years ago, and what appears logical in what I have read. I dare say that many researchers would have to admit to the same practice. I prefer to call myself *a student of the assassination*. Still, if readers of this book find areas of agreement, then I will have accomplished my purpose–to apply some common sense to areas of agreement I have with many writers.

When I first wandered into serious Kennedy assassination reading, it occurred as strangely as finding myself in front of Jack Ruby's Carousel Club on November 22, 1963. Looking for some older books, I called a rather "old and rare" bookstore in Tulsa and was referred to a salesperson, Tom Keith. I went to see Keith, and he started me on avid reading.

Tom, in turn, had entered the field of Kennedy research because, first, he was interested in 1973 and, secondly, he began to find more and more interested persons. Soon he found more than 25, including the researcher. Among us, we had one access to the Twenty Six Volumes in addition to the public library.

When Craig Roberts, an established, prolific author of non-fiction joined us, I am not sure how much he learned from us, but we learned from him. Craig's book, *Kill Zone*, contains voluminous research of his own. To me, it presents the most plausible scenario of the actual assassination presented to date of the killing of JFK.

The group met for 7 years, then separated in a healthy fashion. Each member, writer, researcher or photographer, found his own pursuit and went to work. But we still call each other when we know another holds information we need, and share books.

We are in contrast to the British group, "Dallas '63", which numbers over 100 persons meeting monthly. They annually publish a professional type of journal emphasizing findings and reviews of recent publications. Perhaps that is why we Americans find the British group so refreshing–they're so organized. It will be interesting to evaluate, over a period of time, the progress of the Americans with the British.

Writing strictly for myself, I abhor the squabbles among the American writer/researchers, which is also accompanied by impolite actions and deeds. It speaks ill for the research community.

Outright lies of the pseudo researchers should be curtailed, if we could only convince some major American publishers that it is unethical to publish lies as fact. Not much progress has been made toward that goal.

Some times the Tulsa group met in the home of the researcher for access to the volumes. Owning the volumes does not make one an expert or even a researcher. A researcher is one who has read all the statements and testimony, examined all the exhibits and consulted others in person. Cross checking confuses issues in the minds of persons new to the field, especially when studying testimony of witnesses.

There is one brand of researcher I have encountered which I do not appreciate. There are researchers who have arrived at conclusions which they believe are correct, but refuse to share the elements which led to their conclusions. I don't need to name names; they know who they are. But these people do a disservice to other writers and researchers who many agree with them, but don't dare take their "findings" as fact. Truth should be shared for the common good. *A pox on the hoarders.*

It is also distressing to find volumes which hold theories developed by another writer, and only an original thought of two by the author. That is precisely why *Secrets from the Sixth Floor Window* is two hundred and some odd pages long rather than five hundred.

After finding fault in the people I admire, I reserve to defend them. What an uphill battle they have fought from the time when Lee Harvey Oswald was always described as the killer of President John F. Kennedy until today, when a few encyclopedias insert the word "alleged". What has kept them going? What common bond made them ally even if splitting in the next breath?

Peter Dale Scott gave a good reason in *Deep Politics*. He said, "America's deep politics, like its politics, is partly centralized but also profoundly pluralized, indeed conflicted.....we should look within, not outside, the political status quo, if we hope to understand the assassination." While not all will agree, I endorse his additional paragraph, "The key to a credible model for what happened, through the murders and also the cover-up, is not to think of it as an externalized conspiratorial disruption of our deep political system (analogous to the invasion of an otherwise healthy body an external germ or virus to be isolated). It is to think of it as a synergetic performance by internal ingredients of that deep political system itself."[28]

Twenty Two

Lee Harvey Oswald

Before writing about Lee Harvey Oswald, one of the most mysterious Americans of this century, through his actions as well as his early death, any student must consider his mental state. It is lamentable that no data is available taken during his adulthood. Few adults want to be "judged" by their teenage actions. But that is exactly what the Warren Commission did, and what we are limited to. It is interesting that after truancy in his teens, Oswald was only found guilty of one minor criminal offense–a disturbance while distributing political flyers on a New Orleans street. His other transgressions only received came into the spotlight after he was charged with the assassination of President Kennedy. They were in fact "family quarrels" in which the police were never called.

Thus we are bound only by the sometimes faulty recollections of one physician, Renatus Hartogs, and several social workers. The commentary of the examiner explains: "This short critique of a published psychiatric portrait of Oswald focuses on an assessment of Oswald at thirteen years of age made when he was a resident of New York's Youth House in connection with repeated school truancy." Inferences based on that report are questioned. The author of this section, Dr. Samuel F. Kritzberg, is a licensed psychologist in the state of Oklahoma. He has been in clinical practice for over 25 years and has testified as an expert witness numerous times.

Dr. Kritzberg first quotes from the Warren Commission material on Lee Harvey Oswald.

<u>From the Warren Commission Documents: "Summary for Probation Officer's Report:"</u>

"This 13-year-old, well-built boy, has superior mental resources and functions only slightly below his capacity level in spite of chronic truancy from school - which brought him into Youth House.

No finding of neurological impairment or psychotic mental changes could be made. Lee has to be diagnosed as 'personality pattern disturbance with schizoid features and passive-aggressive tendencies.' Lee has to be seen as an emotionally, quite disturbed youngster who suffers under the impact of really existing emotional isolation and deprivation: lack of affection, absence of family life and rejection by a self-involved and conflicted mother. Although Lee denies that he is in need of any other form of help other than 'remedial' one, we gained the definite impression that Lee can be reached through contact with an understanding and very patient psychotherapist and if he could be drawn at the same time into group psychotherapy. We arrive therefore at the recommendation that he should be placed on probation under the condition that he seek help and guidance through contact with a child guidance clinic, where he should be treated preferably by a male psychiatrist who could substitute, to a certain degree at least, for the lack of father figure. At the same time, his mother should be urged to seek psychotherapeutic guidance through contact with a family agency. If this plan does not work out favorably and Lee cannot cooperate in this treatment plan on an out-patient basis, removal from the home and placement could be resorted to at a later date, but it is our definite impression that treatment on probation should be tried out before the stricter and therefore possibly more harmful placement approach is applied to the case of this boy. The Big Brother movement could be undoubtedly of tremendous value in this case and Lee should be urged to join the organized group activities of his community, such as provided by the PAL or YMCA of his neighborhood."

Comments of Dr. Kritzberg:

<u>The Psychiatric Evidence For The Lone Mad Gunman Theory</u>

The author of Case Closed created a gestalt of selective information in which Oswald is depicted as an emotionally unstable individual, acting as a lone gunman in the assassination of a president. In doing so, the utilization of a psychiatric report on

Oswald when the latter was 13 1/2 years old is underscored by Posner as a significant datum in the motivational picture of the young adolescent who eventually grew up to be the lone assassin of John F. Kennedy.

The use of psychological and psychiatric reports and psychiatric expertise is not new to us but in this case, since the defendant is dead, it would be somewhat difficult to order a second psychiatric examination of the adult Lee Harvey Oswald. Hence, the long chain of motivational causality spanning those ten years of Oswald's life remains very hypothetical.

Neither was the psychiatrist, Dr. Renatus Hartogs, put on the stand to be questioned by a friendly attorney or contradicted in a court examination by a rebuttal witness. The deposition of Dr. Hartogs included within the Warren Commission's data was taken on April 16, 1964, four months after the assassination and the interrogation was performed by Wesley Liebeler, Assistant Counsel of the President's Commission. The doctor was not shown the report which he produced on Lee Harvey Oswald when the latter was a resident of Youth House (New York City) in 1953 until halfway through the interrogation.

Some months before this deposition, Dr. Hartogs had been visited by an agent of the FBI who told him that he was the doctor/ psychiatrist who had done a report on Lee Harvey Oswald. The doctor then began a process of reconstructing his thoughts about Oswald in connection with a seminar given at Youth House in which Oswald was the client under discussion. Hartogs remembered that he had employed the terminology of "potentially dangerous" and "incipient schizophrenia" in his report and also that he had recommended institutionalization for Oswald.

These recollections were creations rather than anything else. When the doctor found they did not exist in his report, after being shown this evaluation, he appeared to be somewhat bothered by his own inaccuracy. However, when Dr. Hartogs admitted that the report "contradicts my recollection", Mr. Liebeler was quite reassuring with the comment "and it is perfectly understandable that it is something that might not be remembered 11 years after the event; I have no recollection of what I was doing 11 years ago".

Dr. Hartogs was well aware of the lone, mad gunman concept. He had been interviewed on a television program some time before this deposition and had been asked to comment on the type of individual who could shoot a president: "I just made some general psychiatric remarks as to what kind of person would kill the president."

"That a person who would commit such an act has been very likely a mentally disturbed person who has a personal grudge against persons in authority and very likely is a person who in his search to overcome his own insignificance and helplessness will try to commit an act which will make others frightened, which will shatter the world, which will make other people insecure, as if he wanted to discharge his own insecurity through his own act, something like that in general terms," stated Dr. Hartogs.

Certainly, the doctor does not seem to have been a devotee of any conspiracy theory at the time of his television interview. In the context of his emotionally disturbed lone gunman orientation, and the absence of the terminology "potentially dangerous" from his report, Dr. Hartogs seems to have been inclined to extend the notion of "passive-aggressive tendencies" to include eruptive and explosive impulses, an extension which would be somewhat questionable in present day terminology and psychiatric classification.

Currently, the diagnostic criteria for "Passive-Aggressive Personality Disorder" utilized by the American Psychiatric Association regards "passive-aggressive" to apply to a "pervasive pattern of passive resistance to demands for adequate social and occupational performance". Oswald's reported acts against his mother, that is, hitting her, would presently be categorized most likely as "Intermittent Explosive Disorder". In any case, beyond the doubtfulness of Dr. Hartogs as a good and reliable witness in this matter, there is the factor of a changing diagnostic system. In 1953, a clear and operationalized system of childhood and adolescent diagnosis did not exist. Indeed, developmental notions about normal and abnormal early adolescence were still vague and unresearched, and mostly based on Freudian theory. Apparently,

Dr. Hartogs was obliged to resort to adult categories in classifying and defining Oswald, rather than utilize the vague notion of early adolescence and adolescent abnormality which then existed.

The terms "schizoid" and "passive-aggressive" are terms which are generally applied to adult character structure, although they can be utilized when adolescent-specific terms do not apply. In 40 years, since 1953, the meanings of such terms as "schizoid" and "passive-aggressive" alone and in combination with each other have been altered in terms of meaning and application. Only in 1968, when the Diagnostic and Statistical Manual of Mental Disorders, Revision Number 2 (DSM-II) was published, did disorders of childhood and adolescence become more separate distinctions from adult pathologies.

In terms of the DSM-II of 1968, the young Oswald would have been designated in one of two categories: either as "withdrawing reaction of adolescence" or "unsocialized aggressive reaction of adolescence".

The concept of "schizoid" which, in addition to abnormal withdrawal from people also implies significant divergence's from realistic thinking and perception would not have been necessary in 1968 and indeed such is not necessarily implied by the Hartogs report.

Mention is made in the report of a desire for "omnipotence" but it is questionable whether this is an unusual trait in an angry young adolescent. Also, it is important to note that even in 1968 definitive criteria for utilizing the above adolescent classifications are absent.

The most recent revision of the Diagnostic and Statistical Manual of Mental Disorders (DSM-III-R) (DSM-IV may be published before this paper is produced/published), does indeed give specific criteria for adolescent disorders, but when the Hartogs report is examined (see Appendix for Summary section of the Hartogs report) in terms of behavioral observations made of the young Oswald, the two "disorders" which now best fit the description of Oswald are "Conduct Disorder" and "Oppositional

Defiant Disorder". Note that in the past, words such as "disturbance", "reaction", or even "illness" might have been used in place of the word "disorder".

With respect to "Conduct Disorder", the description of Oswald in the Hartogs report matches 2 out of 13 specified criteria: #5 -

"Is often truant from school" and #10 - "Has used a weapon in more than one fight". However, the description fits many more criteria within the category of "Oppositional Defiant Disorder":

#1 - "Often loses temper",
#2 - "Often argues with adults",
#3 - "Often actively defies or refuses adult requests or rules",
#4 - "Often deliberately does things that annoy other people",
#5 - "Often blames others for his or her own mistakes",
#6 - "Is often touchy or easily annoyed by others",
#7 - "Is often angry and resentful",
#8 - "Is often spiteful or vindictive".

These eight out of nine criteria match the Youth House description or can be inferred from it. Thus, at the time of the report, using today's nosology, we probably would have concluded that the young Oswald was closer to being an "Oppositional Defiant Disorder" than a "Conduct Disorder".

The course of a "Conduct Disorder" is said to be variable, with many youngsters carrying this diagnosis eventually making a good adjustment to a fairly normal adult existence or one with a minimal amount of anti-social behavior. This depends on whether the "Conduct Disorder" was mild, moderate, or severe. The Hartogs report does not accumulate criteria for the designation of "severe".

Indeed, based on the Hartogs report, the course of Oswald's personality development, would, applying today's knowledge, have been regarded as "unknown", although in many cases the eventuality might have been that of a "Conduct Disorder" or even a "Mood Disorder". The matching criteria suggests that the greatest impairment would have been within the home.

If current day adult diagnostic categories were applied, it is highly probable that the report, in itself, would have elicited the classification of "Borderline Personality Disorder". Some diagnosticians might have utilized the terminology of "narcissistic trends". However, I doubt whether "impulsivity" would have been a major feature noted within the diagnosis.

To the best of my knowledge, none of the criteria in the aforementioned adolescent or adult diagnostic classifications, makes any mention of "smirking behavior" repeatedly noted by Posner in the building of his psychiatric gestalt. "Sulkiness" is about as close a connection that exists in the DSM-III-R and it is found within the definition of "Passive-Aggressive Personality Disorder".

If the reader is confused by all of this psychiatric jargon, that, of course, a major point. The use of a psychiatric report for explaining or predicting an individual's behavior over a 10 year period of time is quite hazardous and should be taken with a very, very large grain of salt. Postdiction is easier. We simply select particular information and emphasize or interpret in terms of conclusions which have already been made.

This does not mean that Posner has made a poor case for an emotionally troubled young adult Oswald. He includes in the building of his gestalt other events in Oswald's life which certainly suggest emotional instability. However, they do not necessarily support the notion of the "lone, mentally ill gunman".

Posner indicates that Oswald, in contrast to being a loner, was attempting to compensate for a deep sense of inadequacy by his later affiliation. Apparently, such affiliations ranged from the United States Marines to pro-Castro communists.

We also have some evidence that such affiliations failed to remain satisfactory for him for any great length of time; attachments became disappointing to him. Rather than a "lone gunman", there is as much evidence that he might have or could have made himself available to a special or elitist group or team. Conceding that there is substantial evidence for emotional instability within the Oswald picture, we cannot see sufficient evidence in the Posner psychiatric data to prove lone and premeditated violence against authority.

He appears to have been an individual who was somewhat group dependent as long as such a group was perceived by him to be special and different. But he seems to have been as equally likely as well as likely to become disappointed and bitter when such affiliations proved to be inadequate to meet his underlying desire for "omnipotence".

The psychiatrically-related evidence supports the qualities of opposition, bitterness, and a desire for specialness, but they do not necessarily support the lone gunman theory. Although Oswald appears to have been relatively incapable of close, long-term attachments, he seems to have been able to affiliate with others on a short-term basis, and even intensely.

The character picture of Oswald is not discrepant from the notion that he could have been strongly influenced by others if they held out the promise of vindication and specialness.

As for Mr. Posner's psychiatric case against Oswald, the emotionally unstable person, we may agree that the probability of this truth is high. To the contention that he was an emotionally unstable assassin who acted alone, the proof must go well beyond the psychiatric arguments themselves. With respect to this contention, I believe that the Scotch verdict "not proven" must apply.

Author's Observations of Lee Harvey Oswald

Lee Oswald was born in New Orleans, Louisiana on October 18, 1939. His father had died of a heart attack before his birth. He had a natural older brother, Robert and a step brother, John Pic. At the time of his birth, if we are to give credence to common psychiatric theory, his mother was quite possibly depressed, which could have adversely affected young Lee. Another factor which would have made his life difficult, was that he did not have a father. Fortunately, once he lived with his brothers his view of "family" could have improved. But nothing can substitute for a father. His brief time with a step father could not fill that void in his life.

Additionally, he may have been dyslexic, as alleged in the book *Case Closed* by Gerald Posner. (p.70) If diagnosed, the disorder might explain Oswald's late school difficulties, except that there is no evidence of a diagnosis by a specialist or even a teacher. Today, there are written and neurological tests for dyslexia, and even treatment. If Lee Oswald did suffer the disorder, it should have made reading in a crowded setting and school tests difficult. Further, while dyslexia is a reading disorder, it can be accompanied by a "developmental expressive writing disorder". If the dyslexic label is correct, it not only explains Lee's spelling errors, but makes him an exceptionally good student. (DSM III-R)

Yet it is well known that Oswald had a love for books so satisfying that he checked them out of libraries and read in quiet, with average comprehension. In fact, in his teenage years his reading was advanced. Many of the books he checked out of public libraries were considered "classics". Even those related to politics required above average reading skills. While his friend, George DeMohrenschildt, contended that Oswald missed the finer points in some of the deeper books, in my opinion, that is to be expected of a teenager reading without the aid of a teacher.

There is no evidence of disruptive behavior by Lee as a child. A famous photo shows a happy curly haired tow-head in a neat sailor suit. He was placed in an institution, where his brothers already resided, for safety and proper supervision. The home was not an orphanage, as children with one parent could reside there if the parent paid tuition. Even Robert found the institution a satisfactory place to live with many activities outside school. They saw their mother at least once a week.

Life was seen differently by Robert and John Pic. The older two lived separately from their mother a great deal of their lives.

Lee was with his mother more of his younger years except for a period of approximately two months when he stayed with his aunt, Lillian Murret. When he was three years old, he joined his brothers at the institutional home, and because of the absence of a string of bad behavioral reports, must have adjusted to the boundaries adequately.

Later, in 1944, when Lee was five, Robert ten and John 12, the family moved to Dallas, Texas. Robert testified before the Warren Commission, (1/274) that they were happy to rejoin their mother. After she married Edwin Ekdahl and began to travel with him in the course of his work, the older boys entered Chamberlain-Hunt Military School in Port Gibson, Mississippi. After a brief year they again began living in an institutional setting. According to his mother, Robert and John's tuition was paid for by his mother. She had received an inheritance of approximately $5,000 from his father.

Lee began a brief period of life with a family and had a dog and other pastimes. Robert remembered that he attended elementary school in Dallas and played ping pong and swam at a recreation center near the school. Even Lee developed hobbies such as stamp collecting, studying the stars at night, and reading when he began his schooling. Unfortunately his stays in a particular school were always interrupted when his mother first moved with her new husband, and even later moved when life appeared better just a move away. Unfortunately, I can identify with that pattern as a young widow. Now I realize I was running from my overwhelming responsibilities, but at the time it all seemed logical. I know the negative affects on my children, and see no way Lee Oswald could have avoided the suffering of adjusting to new schools and friends almost every year. The exception for Lee was the period in the mid 1940's when he lived in Benbrook, a suburb of Fort Worth, Texas. Even his most stable period was marred by the frequent trips taken by the Ekdahls. Lee, no doubt, enjoyed them, but his education suffered.

A few people remember Lee in his teenage years before he went to New York. While a great deal was made of one school ground fight with another student, fighting and truancy was not the problem at that time. Instead, he had a reputation of always having an answer for everything, and began to announce his intention of wishing to travel to Russia and become a writer of short stories. Interestingly, his grades, when in grade school, were well above average. Copies of his report card grace the Warren Commission exhibits.

But Marguerite's marriage ended, with many quarrels about money prominent in the discord. Why Marguerite decided to move to New York is a little beyond understanding, although she placed the reason on the residency there of John Pic. After staying a very few days with John and his wife, she found a small apartment for herself and Lee. Working outside the home again, Lee faced the formidable task of adjusting to New York City. Lee's difficulties with his mother resembled those displayed by many teenagers as they must separate from their mother (and father if one is present), and establish their own identity. Truancy, especially when he lived in New York City, became his most consistent rebellious act. Fortunately for him, there is no indication that he dipped into drug or alcohol abuse. And there are some reasons, though no excuse for skipping school. Coming from Louisiana and Texas, he was suddenly expected to adjust to New York City life. He was teased about his accent by city youths with little or no negative views of themselves. Lee Oswald didn't fit the norm. Rather than ingratiate himself to these strange teenagers, he seemed to make a conscious decision to see what this strange city was like. He conquered the subway system and rode it extensively. He lived near the zoo, and enjoyed not just watching the animals, but studying their behavior. By these teenage years, Lee Oswald had developed the method of learning on his own. It was not necessarily a personality trait, and he was not a "loner" but he was "alone". In his teenage mind, he made the best of it.

Unfortunately the New York City school system did not take truancy lightly, as his mother did. He was placed in the Youth House, where children resided as the result of a great variety of misdeeds. Lee didn't associate with them, which his social workers found unacceptable. It is most likely that Lee Oswald, for the first time in his life was afraid. When his mother visited once, it is reported that he pleaded, "Mother, Mother, get me out of here. There are boys here who have killed people and who smoke".

Fortunately, he was released and off again went the Oswalds, back to New Orleans. At this time Robert had joined the Marines and John was in the Coast Guard. Robert and John established independence in early years and after reaching adulthood, had little to do with their mother. Soon after Lee was accused and killed, they avoided her altogether.

Is there any reason to wonder why, at seventeen, Lee Oswald tried to join the Marines? He persisted until he succeeded. While in the Marines he began to establish an identity. An identity that may leave the conformist in confusion, but to students of Lee Oswald's life, an identity which seems compatible with his upbringing. It is not necessarily that of a killer, but a person who was happiest when he joined others in an uncommon mission.

His personal life was conflicting. His marriage was unhappy, possibly partially due to Lee's outside activities, known and unknown. But his time with his daughter, June, and briefly with Rachel, were exceptionally happy. Always happy when with his own and other young children, Lee also had a demeanor of respect toward strangers. He had his dark side, which became especially apparent to his family after his return from the Soviet Union and he had difficulty holding down a job.

He clearly would not, or could not, abandon the activities which made steady work next to impossible. And that is the part of Lee Oswald's life which, it would seem, has not yet been explained satisfactorily.

Remembrances of Lee Harvey Oswald by his Aunt and Cousin

Warren Commission testimony given by Lillian Murret, aunt of Lee Oswald, and Marilyn Murret, his cousin, give a entirely different impression than is found in the Warren Report.

His aunt's testimony was relaxed, candid, but good natured. She had no agenda, and was obviously not attempting to gloss over Lee's negative actions. She had a good relationship with her sister, Oswald, although Oswald was more opinionated than Lillian. The latter accepted this difference in good grace.

Lillian Murret cared for Lee Oswald in her own home for several months while Oswald worked. It is assumed he slept as well as spent the day at her home, where Lillian had a busy life, raising her own five children. After Oswald went back to work, Lillian testified: "I said, 'Well, I'll keep Lee for awhile you know, as long as I could.' I offered to keep Lee at an age when he was a very beautiful child. Now, I wouldn't say he was smarter than any other child his age. He might have been smarter than some 3-year-olds and so forth, but he was really a cute child, very friendly, and so I kept him and would take him to town, and when he would have on one of those little sailor suits, and he really looked cute, and he would holler 'Hi' to everybody, and people in town would stop me and say, 'What an adorable child he is,' and so forth...."[29]

Lee lived with her from "about 1939 to 1941".

Later, as noted, Lee was placed in the Bethlehem Home with his brothers. Lillian noted that her sister insisted she always paid the fees, as well as future military education of her older sons. While she was married at the time to Edward Ekdahl, Oswald insisted that it was she who provided for her sons.

Mrs. Murret's tenure as Lee's baby sitter eventually ended when his habit of slipping outside and ending up in the kitchen at a neighbors grew impossible for his aunt to cope with. She noted that Lee was not the only child to watch after; there were her own as well.

His aunt also remembered the unusual expression on Lee's face, which writers have called a tight-lipped smile or even a smirk, She testified:

JENNER: What was there about his mouth that you noticed particularly?

MURRET: Well, it was sort of set back a little bit - a little different from most people, but it really wasn't that bad. It just looked like he was holding his mouth that way, but he really wasn't. That's just the way it was, but a lot of people didn't like him for it.[30]

As an older child, she observed, Oswald trained Lee to come home from school and stay indoors to stay out of trouble. Lee listened to the radio and read. She then noted, "When we took him out though, he didn't seem to enjoy himself...he wanted to be in that room all the time."

After living in New York, Oswald returned to New Orleans with Lee. He enrolled in Beauregard school, and had some unhappy moments. Marilyn noted that the kids would call him "Yankee". He was in a few scuffles which usually were started by other boys, one who punched him in the mouth. Marilyn Murret noted the "low standards" at the school. Lee always ate dinner with the Murrets on Friday when they would have sea food, a favorite with him. The next day, his aunt gave him money to rent a bike at the park, which delighted Lee. All in all, Lee's experiences with his aunt were pleasant, almost to a fault. When he had reached adulthood, she tried to press money on him, which he refused.

Lee's cousin, Marilyn, a teacher, noted that she liked Lee. Although she had known him as a student at Beauregard school, she also knew him after his marriage to Marina. She testified to the Warren Commission,[31] "He was very devoted to Marina. He seemed to love his child very much. And as I say, I am saying he was very well-mannered, he really was. And I mean if any other girl sat down, he pulled the chair out, and the car door was opened to let her in and out; he does that for everybody." She thought Lee and Marina were a cute couple.

She remembered a day they went crabbing down by the lake.

Marina nagged Lee the whole time. When Marilyn asked him what Marina was saying, he laughed: "She's telling me that instead of spending money on bait, I should have bought crabs at the market. Just like a woman. No matter what country they come from, they're all the same."

Twenty Three

"Mama" Oswald

Marguerite Oswald suffered enough abuse and neglect in her life that this writer cannot bring herself to add to it in any way. It cannot totally be avoided because Marguerite made herself a public character.

Obsessed or perhaps terrified that she faced a life of isolation and abject poverty, she instead focused on money. After Lee's death, she sold many items for money, and in fact quarreled about it with Chief Justice Warren. In her lengthy testimony is this exchange:

"CHAIRMAN: How much did LIFE pay you for your story?

MRS. OSWALD: Is that pertinent? Or is that my personal business? I think the amount I got would be immaterial to the Commission.

CHAIRMAN: Well, I think it might be material under some circumstances.

MRS. OSWALD: It is not. That is my personal life. It is no crime to sell pictures. I have no job or income. If I want to sell a picture to a magazine or newspaper, and protect myself financially, I am going to continue to do that."[32]

After taking up the personal burden of researching her deceased son's "case", she grew more eccentric. In fact, as time went on, she seemed to acquaintances more and more strange. There were several issues which led to her isolation and estrangement. The authorities, police and federal agents, did not question her about issues of which a mother might have knowledge. She was a pain to them and they chose not to talk to her. That, whether they realized it or not, may have been because of her non-stop manner of speech, especially when under pressure. Author Don DeLillo, captures it his book of fiction, *Libra*, but in a non-judgmental way.

Conversely, author Jean Stafford, mimics her in *A Mother In History*. She typed a tape recorded segment made by Marguerite in the following way.

"...and from then on her husband's a louse. These are the things that just don't jive."

"And now another thing, all the witnesses told how she started complaining about everything as soon as she got here, how she treated him and how she talked about her sexual life and how she denounced him and so on and so forth, and taking up with these Russian people. This is all in black and white. I'm not imagining these things, and thank God there are other people taking this up. I say thank God because there are some people who would like to think that I have hallucinations know it's already been said in the Warren Report. It was said by some attorney. Point blank. 'Do you think your sister'–they said this to my sister–'do you think that your sister has hallucinations?' Why? Because I notice the inaccuracies and coincidences and things that don't jive? I know some people who wouldn't hesitate to make a mental case outa me, and believe me, if anybody's in their right mind, it's Mrs. Marguerite Oswald."

Stafford said that Marguerite paused to let this sink in and take root. "And, as she did so, looked me in the eye," Stafford wrote.

Stafford then quoted Marguerite. "No matter what Marina does, it's news, but locally I can show reporters something in black and white and they won't give me coverage."

I have an acquaintance who knew Marguerite Oswald, after Lee's death, who one day will probably describe her in a befitting manner. It is long overdue.

Twenty Four

Running Scared?

Respected journalist Seth Kantor took flack by insisting that he had seen Jack Ruby at Parkland Hospital, and even talked to him in a casual manner. The Warren Commission didn't believe the theory. Possibly because if true, (which any fellow reporter would believe) Ruby would have time to plant the so-called pristine bullet on the floor or on a gurney, depending on which version is read.

Seth Kantor first thought, as did Jim Koethe and many others, including myself, that Lee Oswald was walking in the direction of Ruby's apartment when he encountered Officer Tippit. We had not had time to hear enough contradictory facts to question whether he could even had reached the spot had he tried. So Commission attorney Belin devised a theory.

That theory, quoted here from Seth Kantor's book. *The Ruby Cover-Up*, was not included in the Warren Commission report because, according to Kantor, "...it was so sound, and made so much sense..." Commission counsel completed it on August 7, 1964, according to Kantor. I quote it indented and probably intact, as included in Kantor's book:

Here's what Belin produced for that draft:

> "The Commission does not believe a substantial inference connecting Ruby and Oswald can be drawn from the fact that Oswald was headed in the general direction of Ruby's apartment, two-thirds-of-a-mile away, when he shot Tippit. Perhaps Oswald was fleeing elsewhere or, perhaps, he was just walking, frightened and aimless. To ascertain another possible destination, the

Commission has examined other evidence for significant signs. One item of evidence that may be more significant than the location of Jack Ruby's apartment is that, when Oswald was arrested, he had in his shirt pocket a bus transfer from the Marsalis bus. After the Marsalis bus left the downtown Dallas area, the only transfer point was at Jefferson Avenue, barely three blocks away from the scene of the Tippit shooting. At the time Tippit was shot, Oswald's bus transfer, marked for 1 p.m. in the downtown area, was still valid, expiring in Oak Cliff at 1:15 p.m., or when the next scheduled bus arrived after the time of issue, if the arrival time was after 1:15 p.m. By walking to the transfer point Oswald could save the bus fare by using his transfer, a not unlikely course of action based on his living habits. There were a number of buses which Oswald could have boarded at the Marsalis and Jefferson transfer point. Walking east on East Tenth Street at the time Tippit approached him, Oswald was taking a direct route to that transfer point, particularly if he wanted to avoid the main thoroughfare of Marsalis as much as possible.

Barely a block away was another bus which could have been boarded by Oswald at Jefferson and Ewing. This particular bus, Route 55, traveled south on Ewing and eventually on Lancaster Road. Since the first Route 55 bus to arrive after 1 p.m. at Jefferson and Ewing came at 1:40 p.m., Oswald's transfer would have been good for that bus. Had Oswald boarded that bus, it would have taken him to a point on Lancaster Road where the first southbound Greyhound bus was scheduled to stop for passengers around 3:30 p.m.

That Greyhound bus could be taken directly to Waco, Austin and San Antonio, Texas, where connections could be made for Corpus Christi, Brownsville, and Laredo, Texas, and Monterey, Mexico. Oswald had just enough money on his person when arrested to pay for such a trip."

The drafted theory never made it into the report...did someone realize they had a bigger problem? The timings made by many researchers that prove it highly unlikely that Oswald could have reached Tippit's location at Tenth and Patton in time to say hello, much less carry on a conversation which could escalate to the point of murder.

Oswald had $13 and change in his pocket when apprehended at the Texas Theatre–barely enough according Commission Counsel David Belin to buy a bus ticket to Waco and Laredo, a beginning of getting to Mexico. Before examining the Belin theory, go back to Oswald's last known sighting before Tippit was shot–at his rooming house. There he reportedly changed pants, retrieved his revolver and donned a jacket. Although he reportedly had worn a jacket to work, he had none when sighted on a bus and in a cab.

At first, it is likely that Oswald walked south for a reason. If it was to be handed some money for his part in complicity, he would likely have gone to the Texas Theatre to meet his contact. In that case, he would have walked due south to Jefferson, turned right, and reached the theatre, never intercepting officer Tippit. If he were going down town in order to return to Irving, as he usually did on weekends, he would have taken a Marsalis bus directly across the street from his rooming house. That bus stop was, in fact, where Mrs. Earlene Roberts, board house housekeeper/manager said she saw him standing.

It is likely that Oswald, if a patsy, was alarmed after the assassination because he knew the FBI was suspicious of him because of his Soviet ties. Agents had visited his home, and had even made a pretext call to the TBSB on at least one occasion.

If not walking toward Tippit, walking south on Beckley to Jefferson, he could easily have seen and/or heard the sirens of over twenty police cars whose drivers were intent on apprehending a cop killer. Oswald then surely became frightened and speedily headed for the theatre. Some have wondered if he would not, instead, headed back to Irving. Even if he believed it would have been safe, he knew that Marina was to spend time that afternoon buying shoes. There would be no one there to let him in.

After apprehension in the Texas Theatre, by six officers Oswald was led to a squad car and taken to the police station. A great deal of attention has been given to Officer M.N. McDonald's statement that Oswald, after seizure, said "Well, it's all over now". C.T. Walker, Thomas Hutson, Bob Carroll, Gerald Hill, (all officers) and George Applin (patron at the theatre) did not hear Oswald say anything, or else, nothing intelligible.

There are even more problems with the Belin theory. The next bus that Oswald could have taken on Lancaster, about a block away, which would have connected with other transportation which could take him to the Texas border, was scheduled for 1:40 p.m. Why would Oswald, who must have known by now that he would be a likely suspect, or have been leaving according to a planned conspiracy, have run on the lam for a bus which was scheduled to arrive forty minutes later a block away? I, for one, will scratch the Belin theory.

Twenty Five

In Captivity

During interrogation by Captain Fritz and others, it is important to note that Fritz did not believe Oswald showed any outstanding outburst of anger, except toward FBI Agent Hosty, with whom he had a history of disagreement.

This is mentioned in several books. However, in *First Day Evidence* by Gary Savage, published in 1993, Oswald was observed by police to be mentally deranged. Some aged officers compare him to John Hinkley, who shot President Reagan in 1981. This version of Oswald's behavior is obviously untrue, even to lay persons who saw Oswald's responses on television.

At one time Oswald said:

"At the time the President was shot I was having my lunch on the first floor."

Quoting author Meagher:

"I have already discussed Oswald's known movements at the Book Depository on Friday morning before the assassination and the testimony of Eddie Piper and William Shelley, who stated that they had seen Oswald on the first floor at noon and ten minutes of noon respectively. The Warren Report does not mention that testimony, even with the usual remark that the witnesses were probably mistaken. I believe that the testimony given by Piper and Shelley has probative value with respect to Oswald's statement that he was having his lunch on the first floor. The Commission has determined that Oswald did not bring lunch to work on that day; however, it made no attempt to establish whether or not Oswald had purchased his lunch. Wesley Frazier testified that some of the men brought their lunch and some bought it at the Book Depository, from a caterer who came around about ten o'clock every morning. In a conscientious investigation, that caterer would have been interviewed, to see whether or not Oswald obtained lunch from him regularly, and whether or not he did so on that Friday."

"It is true that at a later interrogation session, Oswald is alleged to have said that he had brought his lunch from Irving that morning. If he actually said that, it appears to be a falsehood. But there is no transcript of what he said and it would have done no harm to question the caterer and to establish whether Oswald purchased lunch that day. At the same interrogation, Oswald said- according to Fritz-that he ate lunch with some of the Negro fellows who worked with him, one who was called Junior and the other a short man whose name he did not know; according to FBI Agent Bookhout, he said that he ate lunch alone but recalled that two Negro employees had walked through the room, one called Junior and the other a short person whose name he could not recall but whom he would be able to recognize.

The two men described by Oswald appear to correspond with James Jarman, Jr., and Harold Norman. Norman testified that after he had eaten his lunch, he 'got with James Jarman, he and I got together on the first floor'; he had eaten in the domino room on the first floor, and thought that 'there was someone else in there,' but he could not remember who.[33] Therefore, if we assume that Oswald was lying and was not actually present on the first floor, we must acknowledge that by phenomenal luck or coincidence he described two men who were indeed there, although there was no known basis for his expecting or predicting that they would be."

"In further corroboration of Oswald's presence on the first floor of the Book Depository is a document unearthed at the Archives early in 1967 by Harold Weisberg.[34] The document reveals that Mrs. R. E. (Carolyn) Arnold, a secretary employed in the Book Depository, told the FBI on November 26, 1963 that she believed that she had seen Oswald standing in the hallway between the front door and the double doors on the first floor a few minutes before 12:15 p.m. on the day of the assassination."

"It was at 12:15 p.m. that Arnold Rowland noticed a man with a rifle whom the interrogation sessions must be scrutinized with particular care for what they omit, as a basis for evaluating the evidence against the accused."

In her book, *Accessories After The Fact*, Sylvia Meagher presented the entire testimony recorded by Captain Fritz, explaining that they were extrapolated and presented as a single narrative because of each statement's importance and for investigation.

"My full name is Lee Harvey Oswald. Yes, I work at the Texas School Book Depository. I usually work on the second floor but sometimes my work takes me to all the other floors. [Note: Oswald probably said, as other interrogation reports indicate, that he usually worked on the first floor, not the second floor as reported by Fritz].[35] At the time the President was shot I was having my lunch on the first floor. The police officer stopped me on the second floor while I was drinking a Coca-Cola."

"I left the building because there was so much excitement that I didn't think there would be any more work done that day; anyhow, the company is not particular about hours, I don't have to punch a clock, so I thought it would be all right to take the rest of the afternoon off."

"No, I do not own a rifle, but I saw one at the Depository a few days ago. Mr. Truly and some of the others were looking at it."

"When I left work, I went to my room on North Beckley and changed my trousers. I got my pistol and went to the picture show; why? You know how boys do when they have a gun, they just carry it."

"Yes, I was in the Soviet Union for three years; I have corresponded with the Soviet Embassy."

"[FBI Agent] Hosty mistreated my wife on two different occasions; he practically accosted her. No, I have not been to Mexico City. I attended school in New York and Fort Worth; then I went into the Marines, where I finished my high school education. I won the usual marksmanship medals while in the Marines."

"My political beliefs? I have none but I do belong to the Fair Play for Cuba Committee, the headquarters are in New York City. I was secretary of the New Orleans Fair Play for Cuba Committee when I lived there. I support the Castro revolution."

"I didn't rent the room on Beckley in the name of 0. H. Lee. It was my landlady; she didn't understand my name correctly"

"Am I permitted to have an attorney? I would like to talk to Mr. Abt, an attorney in New York."

Twenty Six

Chief Curry

The pandemonium of the third floor Dallas police station on November 22, 1963 was unprecedented. Police Chief Curry, who until mid-afternoon had stayed aboard Air Force One during the inauguration of new President Lyndon Baines Johnson, had not been there to establish order, if it could have been established.

The attendance of the press extended to newsmen and camera crews from throughout America and abroad. During events such as the Olympics months of preparation for coverage is required. The number of press passes are limited and certain press are allowed extended coverage and others limited. No such planning could have taken place in one day. Another factor weighing heavily on Chief Curry was the tradition, supported by the city council, of the greatest possible cooperation between the police and the press. The press depended on it; they utilized it on every occasion. To change the established order would have created more chaos, with every pressman on the rampage. What occurred could not have been avoided, up to the transfer of Lee Oswald to the County Jail.

Testifying before the Warren Commission, the Chief and his Captain of homicide would have been comical if the reader was not aware of their acute feelings of guilt. And perhaps the guilt would not have weighed so heavily if it had been established conclusively that Jack Ruby entered the news group, waiting so eagerly for another look as the accused assassin, by a means which could not have been avoided. Instead, he was there, and ready.

Curry testified that he may have thought of moving Ruby at night, but those arrangements were in Fritz's area, and his choice. In fact, Curry seemed to recall mentioning the possibility but it had been vetoed by Fritz. The Chief said that should they make a move at night, if an attempt was made on Oswald's life, the culprit might escape in the darkness, and finding the newly guilty party would be especially difficult. The Chief did admit that he might have mentioned mid morning as a possible time of transfer in passing to a news reporter.

Fritz, when questioned, became upset at the suggestion that he could have arranged the transfer in a better manner if he had listened to Chief Curry. He wanted no part of it. "Then...if something had happened, it would have been my fault," he said. Reading Fritz's testimony, it would seem that the arrangements were all made by Curry. The arrangements did appear not to have been reviewed Dallas City Manager Elgin Crull. In fact, he so testified.

Few Americans realize what they miss when they have not read Chief Jesse Curry's JFK Assassination File. Curry, who bore the brunt of the killing of Lee Harvey Oswald lived out his days in Dallas. His career was ruined, except that in the Dallas tradition, he was taken care of by receiving jobs and assignments, even that of assuring security. He spoke to the reporters who had not treated him badly after the death of Oswald, and told Seth Kantor that perhaps fate had taken a part.

This man, who most believed was a broken soul, who depended on civic leaders to help him feed himself and his family, would surely write memoirs that held to the "party line". He would surely have contended that if Oswald had lived and gone to trial, his conviction was assured without a shadow of a doubt. But that is not what he wrote. I include it as written for verification.

One section was headed:

Lee Harvey Oswald
Was He The Man?

"The physical evidence and eye witness accounts do not clearly indicate what took place on the sixth floor of the Texas School Book Depository at the time John F. Kennedy was assassinated. Speculative magazine and newspaper reports led the public to believe that numerous eye witnesses positively identified Lee Harvey Oswald as the sniper in the sixth floor window. The testimony of the people who watched the motorcade was much more confusing than either the press or the Warren Commission seemed to indicate."

"Sergeant D. V. Harkness radioed at 12:36 p.m. that he had a witness that said the shots came from the fifth floor of the Texas Book Depository Store. The witness, Amos Lee Euins, had properly identified the floor as the 'floor under the ledge!' - which would have been the sixth floor. Euins, a fifteen-year-old spectator of the motorcade, recalled that before the shots were fired he saw 'this pipe thing sticking out the window.' After the first shot he looked up immediately and saw a rifle with a hand on the barrel and another on the trigger sticking out of the open window. While hiding behind a bench Amos Euins was sure that four shots were fired in all. He had seen at least two of them come from the rifle on the sixth floor."

"About ten minutes after the assassination Dallas Deputy Sheriff Roger D. Craig discussed the shooting with Mr. and Mrs. Rowland. Arnold Rowland had looked up to the Book Depository window and noticed two men standing together in the window. One man was holding a rifle standing with the other man a few feet back from the corner window on the sixth floor. Rowland thought to himself that these were just agents assigned to protect the President. He looked back a few minutes later and 'the other man was gone, and there was just one man–the man with the rifle.' Mr. and Mrs. Rowland were then referred to FBI Agents who interviewed them. No statement about the second man or mention of an accomplice appeared in the FBI report."

"One witness claimed to have seen the sniper from the waist up as he stood with the high powered rifle in the open window. Howard L. Brennan, a forty-five year old steamfitter, watched the motorcade directly across from the Depository. Officers estimated that he was only about a hundred and twenty feet from the sixth floor window. When interviewed at the scene Brennan claimed to have heard the first shot and then to have looked up to see the sniper fire a second shot. Brennan claimed that only two shots were fired from the Book Depository."

"Friday night, November 22, 1963, Howard Brennan watched a police lineup. Brennan was unable to make a positive identification of Oswald in the lineup. He was willing to admit that Oswald resembled the man in the window, but that was all. Brennan's later testimony to FBI Agents apparently varied from month to month after the assassination. Brennan was later to become the Warren Commission's key witness. At the time of the Warren Commission Hearings Howard Brennan was willing to positively identify Oswald as the man he saw in the window."

"Most of the people watching the motorcade at the assassination site were behind it near the School Book Depository. By weight of numbers their testimony carried the most impact. Police investigators still ponder the questions raised by the other accounts. Dr. Malcolm Perry at Parkland Hospital had maintained that the President had been shot from the front. Investigators were awaiting the results of the autopsy with the naive assurance that the government would release a detailed autopsy report which could be used in the investigation. The photographs and autopsy evidence were never released by the government. Apparently portions of the material have even been destroyed. The Warren Commission itself yielded to political pressure and never examined the autopsy photographs."

Are these the words of a broken man? I doubt it. Down, but not out.

Twenty Seven

Captain Fritz

When Captain J.W. Fritz testified before the Warren Commission, counselors were polite, but persisted in greater detail than they had with Chief Curry. Their first quest was to establish that the notes Fritz referred to about Oswald had been made well after the fact.

"MR. BALL: Did someone assist you in the preparation of that notebook?

MR. FRITZ: I had several officers assist with this, and some secretaries. Of course, that helped us out. Of course we worked the whole office ever since it happened so it is hard to say just who helped."[36]

The notes were started after Oswald was killed and added to whenever someone recalled events or comments the suspect had made. No tape recording was made or stenographic notes taken.

Fritz recalled that he first heard that the President had been shot about 12:35 p.m. and waited about "10 minutes" before going to Parkland Hospital "to see whether it was a hoax or whether it was the truth". He then went to Parkland Hospital but then found Chief Curry and suggested that he had best return to the "scene of the crime". That obvious fact seemed to have passed by the chief.

When Fritz entered the book building about 12:52 at the earliest, police were afraid the shooter was still present. "So we, of course, took our shotguns and immediately entered the building and searched the building to see if we could find him."

They started on the bottom floors and worked upward, although Fritz noted that he was frequently called to another area to check out what officers found.

Fritz testified,[37] that about the time the rifle was found Truly told him about the missing employee. He then asked to be driven to city hall to see if the man had a criminal record "and then my intentions were to go to Irving." Of course, he found "his man" sitting in a chair in handcuffs at the police station. He sent others on to Irving and Beckley Street after finding out where Oswald lived. That information was obtained by asking Oswald and receiving an honest reply.

Admittedly, he arranged for a quick lineup. He testified, "I instructed them to get those witnesses over for identification of the officer's (Tippit) killing just as soon as they could, and for us to get a real good case on the officer's killing so we would have a case to hold him without bond while we investigated the President's killing where we didn't have so many witnesses."

Oswald told Fritz he did not stay at the Paine's all the time because Mrs. Paine and her husband were separated and didn't get along too well. In fact, that was why he wasn't going home that weekend.

Fritz felt sure the police employees he placed in the lineup with Oswald were suitable, as soon as they opened their shirts and took off their ties. In actuality, only one had dark hair. Lee Oswald was the only one with a black eye who gave his actual name and where he worked.

Fritz testified that Oswald said, "The only thing I violated was in the show; when I hit the officer in the show; he hit me in the eyes and I guess he deserved it...that is the only thing I have done wrong."

Oswald thanked Fritz for allowing him to use the phone, after at first believing it would not be permitted.

He asked Fritz for an attorney, according to Fritz's testimony.

As to Oswald's demeanor, Fritz testified, "You know I didn't have trouble with him. If we just talked quietly like we are talking right now, we talked all right."

This is quite the opposite of today's old officers who remember that Oswald acted like a mad man from the start.

Fritz seemed to feel that he was on the hot seat about Oswald's transfer. He testified at length:

"MR. BALL: Did you consider transferring him at night?

MR. FRITZ: At night?

MR. BALL: Yes.

MR. FRITZ: Yes.

During the night on Saturday night, I had a call at my home from uniformed captain, Captain Frasier. I believe is his name, he called me out at home and told me they had some threats and he had to transfer Oswald.

And I said. well, I don't know. I said there has been no security set up, and the chief having something to do with this transfer and you had better call him., because—so he told me he would.

MR. BALL: Did you think—

MR. FRITZ: He called me back then in a few minutes and he told me he couldn't get the chief and told me to leave him where he was. I don't think that transferring him at night would have been any safer than transferring, may I say this?

MR. BALL: Yes.

MR. FRITZ: Any safer than transferring him during the day. I have always felt that it was Ruby who made that call, I may be wrong, but he was out late that night and I have always felt that he might have made that call, if two or three of those officers had started out with him they may have had the same trouble they had the next morning.

I don't know whether we had been transferring him ourselves. I doubt that we would use this same method but we certainly would have used security of some kind."

Did Fritz know that Ruby had spent several hours late Friday talking to a off-duty officer in a parking garage? Apparently wanting to establish clearly that he had been in the garage at that time. He had his parking ticket validated that night, a practice he reportedly seldom used.

Fritz complained further about the use of the "money car" (armored car), and newsmen being too close to Oswald during the transfer. But when it came down to saying he could have done it better he would not.

> "MR. FRITZ: Well, I hesitate to say because it didn't work good this way. If I had done it like I would do it or usually do it or something and it hadn't worked I would just be in the same shape you know, and it would be just that bad, so I don't like to be critical of something because it turned out real bad."[38]

One would almost think he knew Ruby would be present however the transfer was made.

Another point avoided by Fritz during Oswald's interrogation was questioning him about curtain rods. He said that was because Marina and Mrs. Paine didn't know anything about it. He avoided showing Oswald the rifle purportedly found on the sixth floor and he didn't want to talk about curtain rods. The size of the sack he used to bring his lunch to work was open for questioning. Oswald said that it was a "lunch sack".

It seems that "curtain rods" bothered Captain Fritz. Why? Could he have not believed Wesley Frazier? It seems strange, but everything that day was strange.

Twenty Eight

The Big Boss

Fritz and others referred to Dallas City Manager Elgin Crull as the "big boss, the man over us all".

They gave Crull a little too much power. Certainly, he made the primary decisions in the running of the city machinery, but he was chosen by the city council. He was a pawn of the politicians. To be sure, he was competent in some areas. The position of city manager is probably the toughest in city management. It carries the most stress and calls for thorough knowledge of many occupations. He has to know how the sewage system works, how the police must be managed, how to acquire property when expansion is desirable. For that reason a good city manager is almost indispensable...almost. Unless he crosses the most powerful politicians. Then he just looks to another city and leaves. Few city managers begin and end their careers in the same city. Any city hall reporter knows the power of the city manager. Most are usually inaccessible to the press.

Crull was no different than the others. When he had all the heat possible as powerful groups canceled conventions Friday afternoon and Saturday, he left town.

Crull went to Lake Texoma and took to the water. He could not even be reached by the police after Oswald had been gunned down. The water safety patrol had to send for him to take a call. He then returned to Dallas, to the home of Mayor Cabell.

There he was sure to be included in doing further damage control. No one will ever convince this former reporter that Crull was out of reach to everyone that night. Using Texas talk, whoever he saw or talked to had to be "mighty powerful". Instead of thinking that Crull allowed the ripples of the lake to wash away his worries is naive. Decisions had to be made. I believe they were.

Twenty Nine

Red Herring?

Addressing the question of time that Lee Oswald resided in Dallas and vicinity leads any writer to consider George DeMohrenschildt, and his wife Jeanne. Were they best friends to Lee Harvey Oswald? Did George get jobs for Lee? Was he a government agent? Was he, as suggested by Jim Marrs, author of *Crossfire,* a red herring?

All of the above? There can be no doubt that George DeMohrenschildt was one of the most colorful as well as tragic figures of the "assassination case".

His testimony before the Warren Commission included the following:

"MR. JENNER: Also, I gather that you are a pretty lively character,

MR. DEMOHRENSCHILDT: Maybe so. I hope so. All sorts of speculation have arisen from time to time. And I don't mind, frankly, because when you don't have anything to hide, you see, you are not afraid of anything...".[39]

Yet, Gary Taylor, his son-in-law, reportedly told the Warren Commission:"...if there was any assistance [to Oswald] or plotters in the assassination they were, in my opinion, most probably the DeMohrenschildts."[40]

Reading George DeMohrenschildt's testimony is frustrating for the student because the man was one of those unfortunate people who often could not remember dates. He remembered a vast number of details, but almost had to place the year by remembering who he was married to at the time. His marriage to Jeanne seemed to be the best of his life, still intact when he died of a shotgun wound to the head, shortly before the House Select Committee attempted to contact him.

A memo by former CIA Director Richard Helms stated that DeMohrenschildt applied to work for the government as early as 1942 but was rejected "because he was alleged to be a Nazi espionage agent".[41] In his testimony, DeMohrenschildt admitted a tie to the intelligence division of France.

"MR. JENNER: Is the name Pierre Fraiss familiar to you?

MR. DEMORHENSCHILDT: Yes; he is one of my best friends.

(conversation deleted)

MR. JENNER: Did Mr. Fraiss have any connection with the French intelligence in the United States?

MR. DEMORHENSCHILDT: Yes.

MR. JENNER: Did you become involved with him in that connection?

MR. DEMOHRENSCHILDT: Yes."

DeMohrenschildt was indeed close to the CIA. He was personally friendly with J. Walter Moore, an agent of the CIA domestic contacts division. Moore and DeMohrenschildt met frequently and reportedly DeMohrenschildt checked with Moore about Oswald. Moore reportedly called Lee a "...harmless lunatic". Before the Warren Commission, DeMohrenschildt said Moore said that Oswald was "okay". What went on that benefited the CIA is unknown, although much has been speculated. George and Jeanne were in Haiti at the time of the assassination, although that, in my estimation, means nothing. Of greater weight is that after George's death, his wife befriended several assassination researchers.

Of Swedish extraction, DeMohrenschildt was an oil geologist. He was an educated, sophisticated individual who knew well placed persons in his early years, e.g. Jack Bouvier. Once in Texas, he innocently worked on an oil rig. Within a few years, he had risen from a rigger to the position of assistant to the president of the American Petroleum Institute.[44]

The flamboyant couple were out and about in Dallas, riding in a convertible, and were noticeably extravagant. On the other side, after DeMohrenschildt's son died of cystic fibrosis, he was deeply depressed. In fact, the incredible journey of the DeMohrenschildts through Central America, largely on foot, was attributed to his need to do something outside his normal existence. "Normal" to DeMohrenschildt would have to be extraordinary to most individuals. They entered Guatemala and were shocked to see American soldiers, Jeanne testified. The trip ended at the Panama Canal. To rest up, they went to Haiti to visit Michael Breitman, a friend of DeMohrenschildt. There he began to cultivate government officials and had received a contract with President Duvalier. The Haitian officials received a letter, ostensibly from the FBI, asserting that DeMohrenschildt was a communist and a friend of Oswald. Commission counsel Albert Jenner assured DeMohrenschildt, "But frankly, I don't think they would do anything like that."

Although DeMohrenschildt had to publicly agree with the Commission attorney, he continued to press for a statement from the State Department that he was not starting any "fly-by-night" operation in Haiti. Jenner gave dim agreement, not promising anything specific.

DeMohrenschildt's first dislike of the FBI occurred when they followed him after his trip to Corpus Christi and Aransas Pass, where he and a lady friend made sketches. The fact that there was a Coast Guard station in Aransas Pass wasn't of interest to DeMohrenschildt. *He was just sketching.* Oh, and maybe taking a few pictures of each other. As George said to Jenner: "Who gives a damn about the coast Guard in Aransas Pass?"

Unfortunately when George began driving toward Mexico, five men who he said claimed they were from the FBI, stopped him, accused him of being a German spy and searched his car.

Jenner pointed out, "I can tell you that is what got you into trouble."

After that the couple proceeded to Mexico and enjoyed their holiday. On his first day of testimony before the commission–April 22, 1964–DeMohrenschildt was confident, frank and even demanding. He and his wife believed that Lee Oswald had cause to fight with Marina, that she was downright lazy and not clean enough with the baby's pacifier. As interesting a person as DeMohrenschildt was, the most interesting aspect of his testimony, is the marked difference he exhibited on the second day–April 23.

On April 22, he testified about Lee Oswald: "Sometimes he was obnoxious. I don't know. I had a liking for him. There was something charming about him, there was some–I don't know. I just liked the guy–that is all."[43] There were other complimentary statements regarding Oswald's Russian fluency and other positive attributes.

Overnight there was a change. It is my belief that something caused him to change his testimony. Negative remarks then began to surface. He said, on the 23rd, "Well, that he beat the hell out of her. Marina told me that he threatened to kill her."[44]

Then he would slip back to statements which in my opinion, were his real feelings. Jenner again asked about Oswald. DeMohrenschildt said, "For instance, he liked animals. My dog was sort of friendly with him. When he would come, my dog would not bark. He really liked walking. He told me that around Minsk he used to take long walks in the forest which I thought was very fine."

Toward the end of his life, DeMohrenschildt obsessed, truthfully or in fantasy, that the FBI was after him, that it wanted him dead. He slipped into psychosis, almost without question.

Author Jim Marrs pointed out in *Crossfire* that he was given questionable medical treatment in Dallas, after complaining of bronchitis. The physician disappeared after two months' treatment of George, and refused to allow Jeanne to accompany her husband. The doctor was never located again.

Jeanne DeMohrenschildt reportedly said that if anything killed her husband other than his own action, it was because he befriended Lee Oswald. It is difficult not to agree with her.

Thirty

Video of My Mind

In the summer of 1993, I began the small task of writing a booklet about the assasssination of John F. Kennedy. I found reconstructing my day (November 22, 1963) on the rewrite desk of the *Dallas Times Herald* far more difficult than I had expected. The three major stories I wrote were vivid in my memory, but not the minutiae of the day. I remembered that I was as busy as anyone in that newsroom, but outside the time I spent interviewing Mary Moorman, Jean Hill, Doctors Malcolm Perry and Kemp Clark, and others on the streets of Dallas, I simply could not recall.

Since then I have talked to other reporters present who remember less than I, but I felt a need to fill the gaps in that day. I called and wrote to as many reporters and editors as I could find, but each remembered only what *they* were doing. We didn't have time to compare notes. I like to think it was a setting of organized chaos, but I'm not positive it was all that organized. Our newsroom scene was certainly more businessslike than the scenes on the third floor of the Dallas police station, but it was still somewhat like flying without a flight plan.

My husband, Sam, a psychologist, mentioned that perhaps hypnosis could help me fill the gaps. He then promply forgot about the matter. I mulled it over, and wished it would help. But I thought not for good reason. Biofeedback never worked for me. Sam had tried to hypnotize me in the past and I remained the hyper-vigilant type A personality I have always been. Control is what I need; control I would never relinquish. The greatest degree of hypnosis I ever attained was deep relaxation.

An internal argument began–should I try hypnosis and make a fool of myself, or give it a chance. Certainly, the day of November 22, 1963, was the most memorable of my life; at least everything I could remember. The rest went by in a blur. Let me make the point that I am aware of what clinical hypnosis is and how it works. Also, I knew that repeated hynoytherapy was not feasible.

I knew the one psychologist who could help me trance if anyone could. That would be Reese Price, Ph.D. who employs Ericksonian techniques. Reese is one of the best. As the summer wore on, I pressed Sam to talk to Reese and see if this very efficient, but busy, psychotherapist would take a chance on me. I wanted *all* that I had once had of that memory. Even Sam will admit that when we first met, over a decade ago, I did not talk much about that dark day. I still smarted from the ridicule of being the only person I knew who believed there had been a conspiracy.

The more interested I became, it seemed the less Sam and Reese thought of the idea. But remember that a reporter must be persistent, even a former reoporter. So they eventually gave in. The day was set. I grew more afraid that I would remain wide-eyed and alert, and perhaps give Reese the thought that he had a manic psychotic in the chair. To make it easier, Reese planned to come to Sam's offfice, where I felt as comfortable as I ever could. It was very hot that afternoon, and Sam and I were at odds over the room temperature as usual. I am heat sensitive and he is not. Sam often wears jackets in the summer when he is with me.

Waiting for Reese, I took possession of the recliner and felt my blood pressure rise as I sat. When he walked in, sat down and asked what I wished to achieve, I was taken aback. I thought he knew, and perhaps he did, but I was required to state it succinctly. I am verbose, not succinct. But I attempted to be as clear as possible about needing to relive that day. Reese had huge, dark eyes that bore into me, and I felt he considered this a hopeless cause. Still, he began the process of helping me trance.

His technique is excellent and I began to relax. Eventually I began to talk about the day and where I was. Sam says I was never in a deep trance. But for me, it was an experience that I would never have expected. After being uncomfortably warm a few minutes before, I grew horribly cold. Ice water could have been in my legs. I asked for cover, and Sam, I believe, placed a woven Indian blanket over me. I reached a point of shivering, and I heard the clatter of the teletypes. "The teletypes, the teleptypes," I said repeatedly. And as I again fearfully heard their warning to the world, I saw the ripped off stories that I searched that day for local news. I remembered who I talked to on the ˙editor's desk–not everyone, but those most important to me. November 22nd 1963, again took form for me. It was never again far in the past, but was rightfully a vital memory of my life.

I knew when the session was over. I had remembered all that I could, at least in one session. Later, I wondered about the coldness, not like any I ever experienced before. Not external, extending inward, like being caught in a blizzard. Instead it was the opposite. Inner fear growing outward. I knew it was not a common element of hypnotherapy.

Sam wondered, with his years of experience, if I was feeling fear that I had suppressed on November 22, 1963. Instantly, I realized that was the answer. That day I was as fearful as the cafe patrons I met in downtown Dallas that night. Something had gone dreadfully wrong, evil was among us.

I think that is what many students of the assassination feel. That is why we cannot give up studying, doing research and wondering. We still strive to drive away the evil that was in Dallas on November 22, 1963. Alas, that can only be achieved by discovering the truth.

Thirty One

Anecdotes

THE REPORTER

Author/researcher Sylvia Meagher–who gave considerable insight into the assassination in *Accessories after the Fact*, wrote: "Normally,I would think, any reporter would have hastened to print the sensational news that Mrs. Hill offered; yet this reporter (Jim Featherston) wanted only to shut her up".

If Meagher had conducted really thorough research, she would have discovered that Featherston, not Featherstone, did exactly what a good reporter should do. He got the picture; he got the story and it was published.

JEAN HILL

A statement made to me by Jean Hill plagued her for years, and bothered me as well. She said there was a "fluffy white dog" between the President and Jackie. She was ridiculed by a number of people, she related, in her story written by Bill Sloan entitled *The Last Dissenting Witness*. I found the statement somewhat embarrassing, and wished I had considered omitting it, but there was no time for reflection. Copy boys were relentless in seizing the paragraphs almost before the period was typed.

Only in 1993 was television news coverage shown which portrayed Jackie Kennedy accepting a small white "Lambchops" stuffed animal which she showed to Jack and carried to the limousine with her. Jean

Hill was vindicated, and I was vastly relieved for both of us when the footage was shown to participants at the 1993 ASK symposium held in Dallas.

Hill had been ill, her father had recently died, and she did not see the comforting clip. On what small and relatively insignificant points of fact reputations rest.

GRACE LINE

George DeMohrenschildt was a friend to the president of Grace Lines, the shipping company used by Oswald to make the first leg of his trip to Russia.

APPENDIX

Appendix A

Illustrations

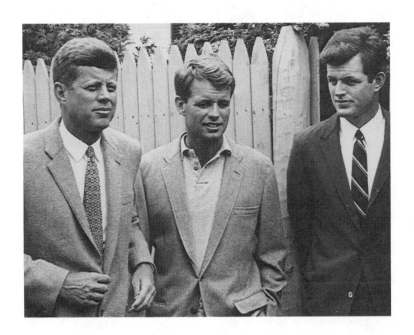

John F. Kennedy, his brothers Bobby and Teddy at the Kennedy compound in Hyannisport Massachusetts. Jack appears somber. The photograph is dated 1960

WANTED

FOR

TREASON

› THIS MAN is wanted for treasonous activities against the United States:

1. Betraying the Constitution (which he swore to uphold):
He is turning the sovereignty of the U. S. over to the communist controlled United Nations.
He is betraying our friends (Cuba, Katanga, Portugal) and befriending our enemies (Russia, Yugoslavia, Poland).
2. He has been WRONG on innumerable issues affecting the security of the U.S. (United Nations-Berlin-wall-Missle removal-Cuba-Wheat deals-Test Ban Treaty, etc.)

3. He has been lax in enforcing Communist Registration laws.
4. He has given support and encouragement to the Communist inspired racial riots.
5. He has illegally invaded a sovereign State with federal troops.
6. He has consistently appointed Anti-Christians to Federal office: Upholds the Supreme Court in its Anti-Christian rulings.
Aliens and known Communists abound in Federal offices.
7. He has been caught in fantastic LIES to the American people (including personal ones like his previous marraige and divorce).

A handbill widely circulated in Dallas on the day of the President's visit was recovered from a street and held as police evidence. It demonstrated the extreme hate some held for the President.

Books for Everyone On Your Gift List! Reviewed in the CHRISTMAS BOOK SECTION Coming Sunday

THE DALLAS TIMES HERALD

FINAL EDITION

CONTINUOUSLY PUBLISHED FOR 87 YEARS — THE TIMES 1876, THE HERALD 1888, CONSOLIDATED 1888

DALLAS, TEXAS, FRIDAY EVENING, NOVEMBER 22, 1963

——JFK Ambushed in Dallas——

PRESIDENT DEAD, CONNALLY SHOT

Johnson Assumes Office

This picture was taken at Love Field on the President's arrival.

LYNDON JOHNSON
Succeeds Kennedy

Grand Jury To Get JFK Slaying Case

Lee Harvey Oswald, the man charged with killing President Kennedy and a Dallas policeman, may not come to trial here before January, Dist. Atty. Henry Wade said Saturday.

Both cases will be presented to a grand jury at the same time, but that likely will not be until the week after Thanksgiving, the district attorney said.

Mr. Wade added that the case resulting from the assassination of the President would likely come up first, although "as the situation now stands, more solid evidence against him is in the slaying of the policeman."

Dist. Atty. Wade said he personally will prosecute both cases, aided by assistants Bill Alexander, Frank Watts and A. D. (Jim) Bowie.

Lee H. Oswald was quickly apprehended and jailed for the murder of Police Officer J.D. Tippit and the President. Saturday he was visited by his Russian wife, Marina. Quickly District Attorney Henry Wade prepared for a Texas grand jury investigation.

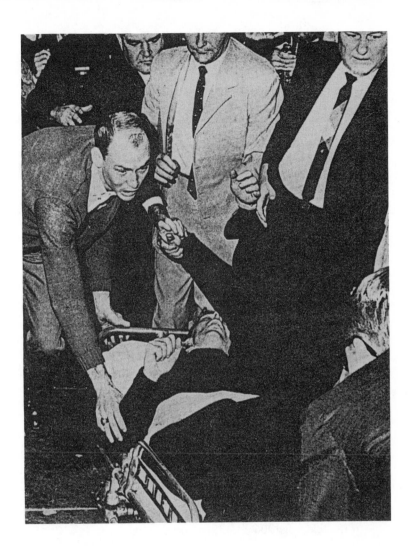

Lee Oswald, shot in the abdomen in the police department basement, is quickly transferred to Parkland Hospital. He died at the same hospital where President Kennedy had been treated and then pronounced dead.

Appendix B

Notes and Credits

Notes

1   *Dallas Times Herald,* November 22, 1963.

2   *Dallas Times Herald,* November 22 and 23, 1963.

3   *Dallas Times Herald,* November 23, 1963.

4   Warren, Leslie, *Dallas Public and Private,* page 12

5   Ibid, page 46

6   Ibid, page 26

7   Ibid, page 85

8   Ibid, page 24

9   Ibid, page 205

10 T.S. Eliot

11 Scott, Peter Dale, *Deep Politics,* page 284

12 Ibid, page 269

13 Ibid, page 206

14 Ibid, p. 286

15 Ibid, p. 288

16 Ibid, p.291

17 Ibid, p. 291

18   Ibid, p. 292

19   Ibid, p. 293

20   7 WH 879

21   Scott, Peter Dale, *Deep Politics,* p. 161

22   Ibid, p. 136

23   Ibid, p. 137

24   Ibid, p.218

25   Ibid, p. 274

26   Ibid, p. 274

27   Ibid, p. 29

28   Ibid, p. 30

29   WH 106

30   8 WH

31   8 WH 172

32   1 WH 274

33   1 WH

34   3 WH 189

35   3 CD 5.41

36   4 WH 234

37   4 WH 234

38 9 WH 169

39 4 WH 234

40 Marrs, Jim, *Crossfire* 200

41 4WH

42 4WH

Photo Credits

vi AP/Worldwide Photos

181 Frank Fallaci, 1960 (John F. Kennedy Museum, Hyannis, Massachusetts)

182 Dallas Police Department evidence. Recovered from a street after the assassination

183 *Dallas Times Herald*

184 *Dallas Times Herald*

185 United Press International photo reproduction

Appendix C
Bibliography

Adelson, Allen. *The Ruby-Oswald Affair*. Seattle: Romar Books, Limited, 1988.

Bishop, Jim. *The Day Kennedy was Shot*. New York, Funk & Wagnalls, 1968.

Blakey, G. Robert and Billings, Richard N. *Fatal Hour*. New York, Berkley Books, 1981.

Bringuier, Dr. Carlos. *Red Friday*. Chicago: Chas. Hallberg and Company, 1969.

Crenshaw, Charles A., MD, with Hansen, Jens & Shaw, J. Gary. *JFK: Conspiracy of Silence*. New York, Signet, 1992.

Davis, John H. *The Kennedy Contract*. New York, Harper Paperback, 1993.

Davis, John H. *Mafia Kingfish*. New York, Signet, 1989.

DeLillo, Don. *Libra*. New York, Penguin Books, 1989.

Dubby, James P. and Ricci, Vincent L. *The Assassination of John F. Kennedy: Dates. Places. People*. New York, Thunder's Mouth Press, 1992.

Duffy, James R. *Who Killed JFK?* New York, Shapolsky Publishers, 1989.

Dulles, Allen. *The Craft of Intelligence*. Washington, The Brookings Institution, 1965.

Epstein, Edward J. *Legend: The Secret World of Lee Harvey Oswald*. New York, McGraw-Hill, 1978.

Fonzi, Gaeton. *The Last Investigation*. New York, Thunder's Mouth Press, 1993.

Garrison, Jim. *On the Trail of the Assassins*. New York, Warner Books, 1988.

Groden, Robert J., and Livingstone, Harrison Edward. *High Treason*. Maryland, Berkley Books, 1989.

Grodon, Robert J. *The Killing of a President*. New York, Viking Studio Books, 1993.

Hayes, Harold, Editor. *Smiling Through the Apocalypse*. New York, Esquire, Inc., 1960.

Hepburn, James. *Farewell America*. Frontiers Publishing Co., Vaduz, 1968.

Hoover, J. Edgar. *Masters of Deceit*. New York, Pocket Books, 1958.

Kantor, Seth. *The Ruby Cover-Up*.

Lane, Mark. *Rush to Judgment*. New York, Thunder's Mouth Press, 1966.

Lane, Mark. *Plausible Denial*. New York, Thunder's Mouth Press, 1991.

Leslie, Y. *Dallas Public and Private*. New York, Grossman Publishers, Inc., 1964.

Lifton, David S. *Best Evidence*. New York, Signet, 1992.

Manchester, William. *The Death of a President*. New York, Harper & Row, 1967.

Marks, John. *The Search for the Manchurian Candidate*. New York, W. W. Norton & Co., 1979.

Marrs, Jim. *Crossfire: The Plot That Killed Kennedy*. New York, Carroll & Graf, 1989.

McDonald, Hugh. *Appointment in Dallas*. New York, The Hugh McDonald Publishing Corp., 1992.

Meagher, Sylvia. *Accessories After the Fact*. New York, Vintage Books, 1967.

Menninger, Bonar. *Mortal Error*. New York, St. Martin's Press, 1992.

North, Mark. *Act of Treason*. New York, Carroll & Graf, 1991.

O'Donnell, Kenneth P. and Powers, David E. with McCarthy, Joe. *Johnny, We Hardly Knew Ye*. New York, Pocket Books, 1972.

O'Neill, Speaker Tip with Novak, William. New York, St. Martin's Press, 1987.

Oglesby, Carl. *The JFK Assassination: The Facts and the Theories*. New York, Signet, 1992.

Popkin, Richard H. *The Second Oswald*. New York, Avon Library, 1966.

Posner, Gerald. *Case Closed*. New York, Random House, 1993.

Roberts, Craig. *Kill Zone*. Typhoon Press, 1994.

Rogers, Philip A. and Craig, John R. *The Man on the Grassy Knoll*. New York, Avon Books, 1992.

Russell, Dick. *The Man Who Knew Too Much*. New York, Carroll & Graf, 1992.

Savage, Gary. *JFK First Day Evidence*. The Shoppe Press, 1993.

Scheim, David E. *Contract on America*. New York, Zebra Books, 1988.

Scott, Peter Dale. *The Dallas Conspiracy: An Unpublished Manuscript*.

Scott, Peter Dale. *Deep Politics in the Death of JFK*. Berkley: University of California Press, 1993.

Shaw, J. Gary. *Cover-Up*. Austin: Thomas Publications, Inc., 1992.

Sloan, Bill with Hill, Jean. *The Last Dissenting Witness*. Louisiana, Pelican Publishing Company, 1992.

Sloan, Bill. *JFK Again: Breaking the Silence*. Dallas: Taylor Publishing Company, 1993.

Smith, Matthew. *JFK: The Second Plot. T.* Great Britain, Mainstream Publishing Company, 1992.

Stone, Bill. *The Other Assassin*. New York, S.P.I. Books, 1992.

Warren Commission Report; 26 Supporting Volumes, in part.

Wecht, Cyril, MD, JD. *Cause of Death*. New York, Penguin Books, 1993.

Weisberg, Harold. *Whitewash*. Harold Weisberg, 1965.

Weisberg, Harold, *Photographic Whitewash*. Harold Weisberg, 1967.

Weisberg, Harold. *Case Opened*. New York, Carroll & Graf Publishers, Inc., 1994.

Wise, David and Ross, Thomas B. *The Invisible Government*. New York, Bantam Book, 1964.

Wolfe, Jane. *The Murchisons: The Rise and Fall of a Texas Dynasty*. New York, St. Martin's Paperback.

Zirbel, Craig I. *The Texas Connection*. Arizona, The Texas Connection Company Publishers, 1991.

Appendix D

Index

Order Form

Secrets

From The

Sixth Floor Window

JFK

Why did the reporters stop?
Dallas in the day of Camelot
Dallas' deep politics
What would a team of investigative reporters find?

'Read all about it' in *Secrets From The Sixth Floor Window*

I wish to order _____ copies of *Secrets From The Sixth Floor Window*.
Please ship to:

Print Name:

Print Complete Address/PO Box/Apt No:

Print City, State, Zip:

Send orders to: Under Cover Press
P.O. Box 703026
Tulsa, OK   74170-3206

$11.95 Per Copy
$ 1.50 Shipping & Handling (Please add $ .50 for each additional copy)
US Currency.   Please allow 2-3 weeks for delivery.